international thai cooking

AUTHENTIC THAI FOOD

By Sisamon Kongphan

Sangdad Books

National Library of Thailand Cataloging in Publication Data

Authentic Thai Food

   140 p.

   1. Cookery, Thai. I. Title.

641.59593

ISBN 974-7160-72-2

AUTHENTIC THAI FOOD

First Published, August 1995

Second Published, January 1998

Third Published, November 1998

Fourth Published, August 2000

Fifth Published, September 2002

Sixth Published, September 2003

Copyright © by Sangdad Publishing Co., Ltd.

Consultant	Sisamon Kongpan
Director	Nidda Hongwiwat
Editor	Nalin Khu-Armornpatana
English Translator	Richard Goldrick
Editor's Assistant	Obchery Imsabai
Photography and Design	Samart Sudto
Marketing Director	Nan Hongvivatana
Production Director	Jiranan Tubniem
Printer	A.T. Printing Co., Ltd.
	Tel. 0-2674-7184

Sangdad Books

Published by Sangdad Publishing Co., Ltd.

320 Lat Phrao 94 (Town in Town)

Wangthonglang, Bangkok 10310, Thailand.

Tel. (662) 0-2934-4413-4, 0-2934-4418-20

Fax : (662) 0-2538-1499

www. sangdad.com

e-mail : sangdad@asianet.co.th

PREFACE

Thai food is becoming more and more popular internationally, gaining recognition as one of the world's great cuisine, because it is delicious, whole some, and easy to cook. To better meet the needs of Thai food admirers in all parts of the world, Sangdad publisher has launched a new series of International Thai Cooking. Under this special series, we proundly present to you Authentic Thai Food carefully authored by Sisamon Kongphan, a leading expert on Thai culinary art.

Sisamon Kongphan currently teaches at the Faculty of Home Economics, Rajamangala Institute of Technology in Bangkok, a post she has held since 1974. Sisamon has spent a considerable part of her career in cookery laboratory where one of her major concerns is systematizing the "pinch-of-this-dash-of-that" sort of measurement so typical of traditional Thai cookery. In her more than four decades as a teacher, Sisamon has had thousands of students, some from far away as Japan and America, and she has reached many more through her video tapes and publications. She is the author of more than twenty cookbooks on Thai as well as other cuisines and contributes regularly to the cooking pages of leading magazines and newspapers. Her recipes are thus accurate and thoroughly tested.

Nidda Hongwiwat
Managing Director

INTRODUCTION

The introduction is divided into two parts. The first describes all the ingredients used in the recipes in this book. The second part is devoted specifically to chilli paste mixtures. These are important because of the extensive use made of them in Thai cookery. A supply of a chilli paste can be made up once,. stored properly in a refrigerator, and used time and again.

MEAT AND EGG

FISH

Rock cod, pla kao, ปลาเก๋า, is also known as grouper, reef cod, and sea bass.

Mackerel, pla thu, ปลาทู, is a small saltwater fish, *Rastrelliger chrysozonus* (Scombridae). Steamed mackerel in small bamboo trays are sold in food shops nearly everywhere in the country; **fresh mackerel,** pla thu sot, ปลาทูสด, are available at the fishmonger's in the market.

Serpent head, pla chon, ปลาช่อน, is the freshwater fish

Squid, *Loligo formosana,* called pla meuk kluai, ปลาหมึกกล้วย, has a tubular body with fins at one end and tentacles at the other. The body is covered with a thin skin flecked with red. After washing, this is removed and the tentacles and head are separated from the body. The clear bone and associated membrane, which are attached to the head, are discarded. Then, the eyes and ink sac are cut away, the hard beak is removed, and the squid is washed again.

Cuttlefish, *Sepia pharonis,* called pla meuk kradong, ปลาหมึกกระดอง, has a flattened, broad,

white body. After washing, the head and tentacles are slipped away from the body, the cuttlebone and the membranes around it are removed, and the preparation continues like that of the squid. It is customary to score it in a criss-cross pattern.

PRAWN

White prawn, kung chaebuai, กุ้งแชบ๊วย, also called the banana prawn, has a white body stippled with minute dots of rust-colored pigment. Fully grown, these prawns attain a length of 20 cm. and more; however, harvesting may begin before they have reached half this. These smaller ones, sorted and priced by size, are sold as kung chihae, กุ้งชีแฮ้, which in the recipes are designated simply as **prawns.**

Tiger prawn, kung kula dam, กุ้งกุลาดำ, so called because of its black and white stripes, is the giant among Asian prawns, the females growing to over 30 cm. long. Pond rearing of tiger prawns was more recently established than that of the white prawn but is very promising.

Dried shrimp, kung haeng, กุ้งแห้ง, are small shrimp which have been dried in the sun.

EGG

Salted eggs, khai khem, ไข่เค็ม, are duck eggs preserved by soaking in brine for a month or so.

RICE AND FLOUR

Rice noodles, kui tiao, เส้นก๋วยเตี๋ยว, are flat white noodles made from rice flour and are cut into strips of three widths:wide (2-3 cm.), sen yai, เส้นใหญ่, narrow (about 5 mm.), sen lek, เส้นเล็ก, and thin (1-2 mm.), sen mi, เส้นหมี่, Uncut fresh noodle sheets are sold in the market, as are fresh wide and narrow rice noodles. Thin noodles are available dried, and wide and narrow noodles may also be bought in this form, Dried noodles are soaked in water before use to soften them.

Vermicelli, knanom jeen, ขนมจีน, are thin, round noodles, also made from rice flour, and sold fresh in the form of wads that look like birds' nests. They should be eaten within a few days of being made, and it is a good practice to steam them after bringing them home from the market.

Mungbean noodles, woon sen, วุ้นเส้น, are thread-like noodles made from mung bean flour. They are sold dried and are soaked in water before use. When cooked, they become transparent. High quality noodles maintain their integrity in soup better than do cheap ones.

Rice flour, paeng khao jaao, แป้งข้าวเจ้า, is made from nonglutinous rice.

Tapioca pellets, sa-khu met lek, สาคูเม็ดเล็ก, are the tiny balls (about 2 mm.in diameter) made from tapioca, some used in sweets. They should be mixed with hot, but not scalding, water and kneaded, and then allowed to stand for a time covered with a damp cloth to permit the water to penetrate to the core.

SEASONING SAUCE

Fish sauce, nam pla, น้ำปลา, is a clear, brown liquid derived from a brew of fish or shrimp mixed with salt. It is sold in bottles and plastic jugs as well as in earthenware jars. High quality fish sauce has a fine aroma and taste. Fish sauce is placed on the table as a condiment at nearly every meal, either as is or mixed with sliced chillies and perhaps lime juice.

Light soy sauce, si-iu khao. ซีอิ๊วขาว, is a clear brown, liquid used in much the same way that fish sauce is.

Fermented soybeans, tao jiao, เต้าเจี้ยว, is a brew of soybeans and salt.

Palm sugar, nam tan pip, น้ำตาลปีบ, was originally made from the sap of the sugar, or palmyra, palm, *Borassus flabellifera,* called tan in Thai, which has a very rough trunk and large, fan-shaped leaves. Now it is generally made from the sap of coconut plams, and may be sold as coconut sugar. The sugar is a light golden brown paste with a distinctive flavor and fragrance. It is put up in five-gallon kerosene cans, called pip in Thai.

Shrimp paste, ka-pi, กะปิ, is shrimp which are salted, perhaps brewed for a time, allowed to dry in the sun, then ground and worked with the addition of moisture into a fine-textured puce paste, which is fragrant and slightly salty.

Beancurd, tao hu, เต้าหู้, is made up salted and unsalted in solid and soft forms. The solid curd has a cheesy consistency and is sold in blocks about four inches square. The blocks of the unsalted curd are white while those of the salted, **yellow beancurd,** tao hu leuang, เต้าหู้เหลือง, are yellow on the outside and off-white inside. The solid curd is used in fried dishes. The **soft white beancurd,** tao hu khao chanit on, เต้าหู้ขาวชนิดอ่อน, is cut into bricks for sale and is used in soups.

HERBS AND SPICES

Shallot, hom lek, หอมเล็ก, or hom daeng, หอมแดง, *Allium ascalonicum,* is the zesty small red onion flavored in Thai cooking.

Spring shallot, ton hom, ต้นหอม, *Allium fistulosum,* also called green onion or scallion, has leaves that are circular in cross section. These are much used as a garnish. The bases of the plant are frequently served on the side of one-dish meals, such as fried rice, or placed on the salad plate.

Hot chillies, phrik khi nu, พริกขี้หนู, are the

hottest type and also the smallest, being only about a centimeter long.

Spur chilli, phrik chi fa, พริกชี้ฟ้า, have plump lang-like fruits 7-12 cm. long. The green immature fruits become red, orange, or yellow when ripe. Hot.

Dried chilli, phrik haeng, พริกแห้ง, is fully ripened, red spur chillies dried either in the sun or by smoking. They may be large or small, depending on the variety of spur chilli used. They are prepared by removing the seeds, soaking in water, and then pounding in a mortar. Bright red dried chillies should be selected for the color they lend chilli pastes. Smoked chillies are darker in color.

Galangal, kha, ข่า, *Alpinia galangal,* is a largar and lighter-colored relative of ginger and has its own distinctive taste.

Lemon grass, ta-khrai, ตะไคร้, *Cymbopgon citratus,* is an aromatic grey-green grass. The bases of the stems are used in cookery.

Kaffir lime, ma-krut, มะกรูด, *Citrus hystrix,* has green fruits with wrinkled skin. The rind and the leaves are used in cookery.

Wild ginger, Kra-chai, กระชาย, *Kaempferia panduratum,* grows bunches of slender and short yellow-brown tuberous roots and is used in fish dishes.

Ginger, khing, ขิง, *Zingiber officinale,* grows from an underground stem, or rhisome. Mature ginger stems are buff colored; **young or fresh ginger,** khing on, ขิงอ่อน, is white and is eaten fresh and pickled as well as cooked.

Tumeric, kha-min, ขมิ้น, *Curcuma longo,* is a small ginger with brown rhisomes. Tnside, the flesh is a bright carrot orange. An important use is as a coloring agent.

Sweet basil, horapha, โหระพา, is an attractive plant with deep green leaves and often reddish stems. It has a taste reminiscent of anise.

Holy Basil, ka-phrao, กะเพรา, There are two types of holy basil, light and dark, the latter being dark purple. The dark type in fragrant when heated. Holy basil is also eaten fresh. Light holy basil is not used much except in spicy salads because they are not so fragrant. With a slightly hot flavor, though not so hot as pepper, holy basil leaves are used in many Thai dishes, including stir-fried meat dishes and curries.

Sweet basil, maenglak, แมงลัก, is a bright light green plant with a tangy taste.

Mint leaves, sa-ra-nae, สะระแหน่, Thai mint leaves, are round, not thick, hairless, and slightly wavy. The stem tends to be dark red. It is easy to grow, and Thais commonly plant it in pots kept near the kitchen, where it can always be easily gathered.

Coriander, phak chi, ผักชี, *Coriandrum sativum,* is of the parsley family. The leaves and stems are eaten fresh and used frequently as a garnish. The root and the seeds are ingredients in many dishes. The root is taken from the fresh plant. The seeds which are roughly spherical, 2-4 cm. in diameter, and range in color from off-white to brown, have a pleasant taste and fragrance. They can be bought in the market. It is better to roast and grind seeds immediatly

before use than to buy ground coriander seed.

Pandanus leaf, bai toey, ใบเตย, *Pandanus odorus,* the long, bright green leaf of a small palm and is used in making sweets.

Cumin, yee-ra, ยี่หร่า, *Cuminium cyminum,* has elongated yellow-brown seeds about 5 mm.in length, which are ridged longitudinally and often have a seed stalk attached. They are roasted before use to heighten their fragrance.

Cinnamon, ope-choey, อบเชย, *Cinna-momun spp.,* is the bark of a number of species of trees in this genus, classified in the laurel family. The types that grow in Southeast Asia are known in commerce as cassias. The barks, which are generally reddish-brown, after being peeled off from around the branch, tend to roll themselves back up, and so have a scroll-like appearance. For retail sale in Thai markets, the bark is cut into strips about 1 cm. across and 8-10 cm. long, and such strips are the basis for the measurements given in the recipes. Before use, the bark should be roasted to bring out its aroma.

Cardamoms, luke kra-wan, ลูกกระวาน, *Amo-mum kreuanh,* appear like miniature, unhusked coconuts. The off-white, bulb-shaped capsules reach about 1 cm. in length and slightly more than this diameter. Inside is a densely-packed cluster of angular, dark brown seeds, which are aromatic and have a slightly hot taste.

VEGETABLES AND FRUITS

Wax gourd, fuk khiao, ฟักเขียว, *Benincasa* *hispida,* also called white gourd or Chinese preserving melon, is oblong and light green to white. The ends are rounded and the flesh is solid and white.

Sponge gourd, buap liam, บวบเหลี่ยม, *Luffa acutangula,* also called vegetable gourd or Chinese okra, is oblong, pointed, and dark green and has sharp longitudinal ridges.

Bottle gourd, nam tao, น้ำเต้า, *Lagenaria leucantha,* has a rounded body from which arises a straight, narrow neck. The young green gourd is used as food.

Gord gourd, phak dumleung, ผักตำลึง, *Coccina indica,* is a small vine bearing a cu-cumber-like fruit which turns red when ripe. The tips of the vines and the young leaves are used in soups.

Phak wan, phak wan, ผักหวาน, *Melientha suavis,* is a forest tree whose young leaves and flowers are much relished.

Banana,Nam Wa, kluai nam wa variety, กล้วยน้ำว้า, *Musa sapientum,* probably the most popular eating banana among the nearly thirty varieties found in Thailand, has short ablong fruits that become a pale yellow as they ripen. The leaf, bai tong, ใบตอง, of this variety is used.

Ma-kheua phuang, มะเขือพวง, *Solanum torvum,* grow in clusters and, when yet unripe, look like large peas.

Eggplant, ma-kheua, มะเขือ, *Solanam spp.,* are eaten with nam phrik. There are a number of types, ranging in size from that of a ping-pong ball down to that of a marble, in shape from that of an egg to that of a flattened sphere, and in color from green and white to yellow.

One small type is called **ma-kheua pro,** มะเขือเปราะ

Long eggplant, ma-kheua yao, มะเขือยาว, has a long green fruit.

Ma-euk, มะอึก, *Solanum Ferox,* is an eggplant having a furry fruit with a sour taste, The hairs are scraped off before use.

Bean sprouts, thua ngok, ถั่วงอก, are usually sprouted mungbeans. The seed husk and the stringy end of the sprout are removed before use.

Celery, kheun chai, ขึ้นฉ่าย, *Apium graveolens,* also called celeriae, turniprooted celery, or Chinese soup celery, has very small stalks (only a few millimeters across) and a very strong flavor.

Swamp cabbage, Phak bung, ผักบุ้ง, *Ipomoea aquatica,* also called water convolvulus, water spinach, or aquatic morning glory, has hollow stems and roughly triangular leaves. The Thai variety has

delicate dark green leaves and deep red stalks white the Chinese is thicker, larger, and lighter green, The tender tips of the stems are eaten fresh or cooked.

Chinese radish, phakkat hua, ผักกาดหัว, or hua chai thao, หัวไชเท้า, *Raphanus sativus* (long-pinnatus variety), has a long, cylindrical root that looks like a hefty white carrot.

Mushrooms, het, เห็ด, of many types are available fresh. The common are the **rice straw mushroom,** het fang, เห็ดฟาง, the **angel mushroom,** het nang fa, เห็ดนางฟ้า, the **oyster mushroom,** het nang rom, เห็ดนางรม, the **abalore mushroom,** het pao heu, เห็ดเป๋าฮื้อ, These many types of cummonly used mushroom could be substituted for one

another in cooking, if necessary.

Ear mushroom, het hu nu, เห็ดหูหนู, is a dark greyish brown fungus that has a delightful crunchy texture.

Shiitake mushroom, het hom, เห็ดหอม, is available dried in the market.

Bitter gourd, ma-ra, มะระ, *Momordica charantia,* also called bitter cucumber, carilla fruit, or balsam pear, is an oblong fruit, pointed at one end, which has a handsome pale green surface covered with an irregular pattern of ridges. There are also small dark green varieties. The young leaves and shoots are also eaten. All are bitter to the taste.

Chinese chives, ton kui chai, ต้นกุยช่าย, *Allium tuberosum,* looks something like spring shallot. The leaves, however, are solid, flat, and fairly thick. The stem and lower part of the leaves are served on the side of dishes such as phat thai, and the chopped leaves are used as a garnish.

Tamarind, ma-kham, มะขาม, *Tamanindus indica,* is a tree which bears tan pods inside of which are bean-like hard brown seeds surrounded by sticky flesh. The tan pod shell can be removed easily, **Ripe tamarind,** ma-kham piak, มะขามเปียก, is the flesh, seeds, and veins, of several fruit pressed together in the hand to form a wad.

CURRY PASTE

NAM PHRIK KAENG KHUA
(Kaeng Khua Curry Paste)

INGREDIENTS
5	dried large chillies, seeds removed and soaked in water
5	shallots
2	garlic bulbs
1	tsp. finely sliced galangel
1	tbsp. finely sliced lemon grass
1	tsp. salt, 1 tsp. shrimp paste

Pound or blend all ingredient until ground

NAM PHRIK KAENG KA-RI
(Yellow Curry Paste)

INGREDIENTS
3	dried chillies, seeds removed, soaked in water
5	broiled shallots
10	broiled garlic cloves
1	tsp. sliced galangal
1	tbsp. lemon grass
1	tsp. broiled ginger
1	tbsp. roiled coriander seeds
1	tsp. roasted comin seeds
2	tsp. curry powder
1	tsp. salt
1	tsp. shrimp paste

Pound or blend all ingredient until ground

NAM PHRIK KAENG MATSAMAN
(Matsaman Curry paste)

INGREDIENTS
3	driec chillies, seeds removed, soaked in water
5	roasted shallots
2	roasted garlic bulbs
1	tsp. minced roasted galangal
1	heaping tbsp. thinly sliced roasted lemon grass
2	cloves, roasted and ground
1	tbsp. ground roasted coriander seeds
1	tsp. ground roasted cumin seeds
5	pepper corns
1	tsp. salt
1	tsp. shrimp paste

Pound or blend all ingredient until ground

NAM PHRIK KAENG KHIAO WAN
(Green Curry Paste)

INGREDIENTS
15	green hot chillies
3	tbsp. chopped shallots
1	tbsp. chopped garlic
1	tsp. chopped galangal
1	tbsp. chopped lemon grass
1/2	tsp. chopped kaffir lime rind
1	tsp. chopped coriander root
5	pepper corns
1 1/2	ground roasted criarder seeds
1/2	tsp. ground roasted cumin seeds
1	tsp. shrimp pastc
1	tsp. salt

Pound or blend all ingredient until ground

NAM PHRIK KAENG DAENG
(Red Curry Paste)

INGREDIENTS
13	small dried chillies, seeds removed, soaked in water
3	tbsp. chopped shallot
4	tbsp. chopped garlic
1	tbsp. chopped galangal
2	tbsp. chopped lemon grass
2	tsp. chopped kaffir lime rind
1	tbsp. chopped coriander root
20	pepper corns
1 1/2	tsp. ground roasted criander seeds
1/2	tsp. ground roasted cumin seeds
1	tsp. shrimp paste
1	tsp. salt

Pound or blend all ingredient until ground

CONTENTS

56. PHAD PHAK RUAM MID
Stir-fried asparagus, carrot, and
cauliflower with mushrooms

58. PHAD PHED KUNG
Stir-fried prawn with red curry paste

60. PLA KAO RAD PHRIK KAENG
Fried grouper with chilli sauce

62. KHAI JIAO MU SAB
Ground pork omelette

64. THOD MUN PLA
Fried fish cakes

66. KAI HO BAI TEUI
Fried chicken wrapped with pandanus leaf

SPICY SALAD DISHES

68. YAM THALE
Sour and spicy seafood salad

70. YAM WUN SEN
Spicy mungbean noodle salad

72. YAM HED FANG
Sour and spicy mushroom salad Thai style

74. YAM NEUA YANG
Barbecued beef salad Thai style

76. YAM MA-KHEUA YAO
Savory long eggplant

78. NAM PHRIK LONG RUA LAE-MU WAN
Sweet pork with hot chilli sauce

80. NAM PHRIK ONG
Pork and tomato sauce

82. NAM PHRIK KAPI
Shrimp paste chilli sauce with vegetable

84. LON HAM
Rice picble ham in coconut cream

ONE-PLATE DISHES

86. KHANOM JEEN NAM PHRIK
Rice vermicelli and sweet prawn sauce

88. KHANOM JEEN NAM YA
Rice vermicelli with fish sauce

90. PHAD THAI KUNG SOD
Fried noodles Thai style

92. MEE KATI
Rice noodle in coconut milk sauce

94. PHAD MEE KROB
Crispy sweet and sour rice noodles

96. KHAO MU THOD KRATHIAM
PHRIK THAI
Pork marinated in garlic fried and
pepper on rice

98. KHAO PHAD KA-PHRAO MU
Spicy pork fried rice on crispy basil
leaves

100. KHAO PHAD SEE MUANG
Stir-fried rice with shrimp paste

102. KHAO PHAD MU REU KUNG SAI
KHAI
Fried rice with pork or shrimp and egg

THUNG THONG
Golden bags
ถุงทอง

INGREDIENTS

30 spring roll sheets cutted, 5 inch diameter
1 cup ground prawn, 1/2 cup ground pork
1/4 cup small chunks yam bean tuber
1 tbsp. finely pounded coriander root
1 tbsp. finely pounded garlic
1/4 tsp. ground pepper, 1 tsp. salt
1/4 cup cooking oil for stir frying
4 cups cooking oil for deep frying
1/2 cup sweet sauce

PREPARATION

1. Mix the shrimp and pork together with all ingredients, except spring roll sheet and chopped garlic.

2. Heat the oil for stir frying in a wok. When hot, put in the chopped garlic, sauté until fragrant, and then put in the filling mixture from Step 1 and stir fry until done.

3. On each the spring roll sheets, place 1 tbsp. of the filling, and then fold up the sheet to enclose as in a bag. Tie the bag closed with a strip of any kind vegetable stalk, made by scalding the stalks in boiling water and then dividing the stalks into strips. The bag should fit tightly around the filling. Trim the excess spring roll sheet and vegetable stem with scissors to make the bags attractive.

4. Heat the 4 cups of oil in a deep wok. When hot, deep fry the bags until golden ; then remove from the wok, drain, and serve with a sweet sauce.

เครื่องปรุง

แป้งเปาะเปี๊ยะแผ่นเล็ก
เส้นผ่าศูนย์กลาง 5 นิ้ว 30 แผ่น
กุ้งบด 1 ถ้วย
หมูบด 1/2 ถ้วย
มันแกวหั่นชิ้นเล็ก 1/4 ถ้วย
รากผักชีโขลกละเอียด 1 ช้อนโต๊ะ
กระเทียมโขลกละเอียด 1 ช้อนโต๊ะ
พริกไทยป่น 1/4 ช้อนชา
เกลือป่น 1 ช้อนชา
น้ำมันสำหรับผัด 1/4 ถ้วย
น้ำมันสำหรับทอด 4 ถ้วย
น้ำจิ้มหวาน 1/2 ถ้วย

วิธีทำ

1. ผสมกุ้ง หมูบดกับเครื่องปรุงทั้งหมดเข้าด้วยกัน ยกเว้นกระเทียมสำหรับเจียว

2. ใส่น้ำมันสำหรับผัดลงในกระทะ ใส่กระเทียมเจียว พอหอม ใส่เครื่องที่ผสมไว้แล้ว (ส่วนผสมข้อ 1) ลง ผัด พอสุก ตักใส่จาน

3. ตักไส้ใส่ประมาณ 1 ช้อนโต๊ะ แล้วจึงจับรวบขึ้น ผูกด้วยขึ้นฉ่ายที่จักเป็นเส้น ลวกน้ำร้อน ใช้เป็น เชือกผูกให้แน่น แต่งให้สวย โดยใช้กรรไกรตัดส่วน ที่เกินออกบ้าง

4. ใส่น้ำมันสำหรับทอดลงในกระทะ พอน้ำมันร้อน ใส่ถุงทองทอดให้เหลือง ตักขึ้นให้สะเด็ดน้ำมัน เสิร์ฟ กับน้ำจิ้มหวาน

POH PIAH THOD

Egg rolls (Spring Rolls)

เปาะเปี๊ยะทอด

INGREDIENTS

300 grams small spring roll sheets
1 cup chopped pork
1 egg
25 grams mungbean noodles
1 cup finely sliced cabbage
1 cup bean sprouts
1 tbsp. chopped garlic
1/2 cup wheat flour paste
(mix 2 tbsp. wheat flour in 1/4 cup water
and stirring over low heat)
1/4 tsp. ground pepper
1 tbsp. light soy sauce
3 cups cooking oil for frying
1 cup sweet sauce

PREPARATION

1. Soak noodles until soft, then cut into short lengths. Mixed pork, egg, cabbage, bean sprouts and light soy sauce and noodles together.

2. Fry the garlic in some oil and then add the pork and noodle mixture. Fry until fairly dry, then dip up.

3. Place a tbsp. of filling on an spring roll sheet, fold the sheet over the filling, roll about half a turn, fold in the ends to close them, then roll up tightly, with wheat flour paste. Deep fried low heat until crisp and golden brown. Serve with sweet sauce, cucumber, and sweet basil leaves.

เครื่องปรุง

แป้งเปาะเปี๊ยะแผ่นเล็ก 300 กรัม
หมูสับ 1 ถ้วย
ไข่ไก่ 1 ฟอง
วุ้นเส้น 25 กรัม
กะหล่ำปลีหั่นฝอย 1 ถ้วย
ถั่วงอก 1 ถ้วย
กระเทียมสับ 1 ช้อนโต๊ะ
แป้งเปียก 1/2 ถ้วย
(แป้งสาลี 2 ช้อนโต๊ะ น้ำ 1/4 ถ้วย กวนพอสุก)
พริกไทยป่น 1/4 ช้อนชา
ซีอิ๊วขาว 1 ช้อนโต๊ะ
น้ำมันสำหรับทอด 3 ถ้วย
น้ำจิ้มหวาน 1 ถ้วย

วิธีทำ

1. แช่วุ้นเส้นพอนุ่ม ตัดท่อนสั้นๆ ผสมเนื้อหมู ไข่ กะหล่ำปลี ถั่วงอก พริกไทย ซีอิ๊วขาว ให้เข้ากัน ใส่วุ้นเส้น คลุกให้เข้ากัน

2. เจียวกระเทียม ใส่ส่วนผสมข้อ 1 ลงผัดพอสุกแห้ง ตักขึ้น พักไว้ให้เย็น

3. ตักไส้ใส่ในแผ่นแป้ง 1 ช้อนโต๊ะ ม้วนพับหัวท้าย ม้วนให้แน่นทาแป้งเปียก ทอดในน้ำมันมาก น้ำมันร้อนๆ ไฟอ่อน ทอดจนเหลืองกรอบ เสิร์ฟกับน้ำจิ้มและแตงกวา โหระพา

LA TIANG

Mixed pork and shrimp in egg net

ล่าเตียง

INGREDIENTS

1 cup ground pork

1/2 cup ground fresh shrimp

6 eggs, beaten

1/4 cup coriander leaves

2 thinly sliced red spur chillies

1 tbsp. well pounded mixture of coriander root, pepper, and garlic

1/2 cup ground roasted peanuts

1/4 cup diced onion

3 tbsp. sugar

3 tbsp. fish sauce

2 tbsp. cooking oil

เครื่องปรุง

หมูบด 1 ถ้วย

กุ้งสดบด 1/2 ถ้วย

ไข่ตีพอเข้ากัน 6 ฟอง

ผักชีเด็ดเป็นใบ 1/4 ถ้วย

พริกชี้ฟ้าแดงหั่นฝอย 2 เม็ด

รากผักชี พริกไทย กระเทียม

โขลกละเอียด 1 ช้อนโต๊ะ

ถั่วลิสงคั่วป่น 1/2 ถ้วย

หอมใหญ่หั่นสี่เหลี่ยมเล็ก ๆ 1/4 ถ้วย

น้ำตาลทราย 3 ช้อนโต๊ะ

น้ำปลา 3 ช้อนโต๊ะ

น้ำมัน 2 ช้อนโต๊ะ

PREPARATION

1. Fry coriander root mixture until fragrant, add pork and fry until done, then add shrimp and onion and then fish sauce and sugar. Add the peanuts and continue frying, until dry.

2. Spread thin layer of oil over entire inner surface of a frying and place on low heat. When hot, dip fingers into egg, then slightly spread, quickly move hand, allowing thin streams of egg to fall onto the pan. Continue in this way crisscrossing the pan to make a net. When egg is cooked, remove from pan.

3. Place the egg net down so the smooth side is on the bottom. Make across with sliced red spur chilli in the center, then put on the coriander leaves, and finally the pork filling. Then fold up into a square as in the picture, and serve.

วิธีทำ

1. ใส่น้ำมันลงในกระทะ ตั้งไฟ ใส่เครื่องที่โขลกผัด ให้หอม ใส่เนื้อหมู ผัดพอสุก ใส่กุ้ง หอมใหญ่ ปรุง- รสด้วยน้ำปลา น้ำตาล ใส่ถั่วลิสง ผัดให้เข้ากันพอ แห้ง ยกลง

2. ทาน้ำมันให้ทั่วกระทะ ตั้งไฟอ่อน พอกระทะร้อน ใช้นิ้วจุ่มในไข่สะบัดลงในกระทะเป็นตารางทำให้เป็น แผ่น ๆ พอสุกตักขึ้น

3. วางแผ่นไข่ที่เป็นตารางทางด้านเรียบให้อยู่ทาง ด้านล่าง วางพริกชี้ฟ้าแดงให้เป็นรูปกากบาทตรง กลางแผ่นไข่ วางผักชี ตักไส้ที่ผัดไว้ ใส่ห่อให้เป็น รูปสี่เหลี่ยม

SA-KHU SAI MU

Flower dumpling filling in mined pork and shrimp

สาคูไส้หมู

INGREDIENTS

1 1/2 cup small tapioca pellets
1 cup chopped pork
1 cup chopped onion
1/2 cup ground roasted peanuts
4 garlic cloves
1/2 tsp. pounder coriander root
3 tbsp. fried garlic (for topping)
1/4 tsp. ground pepper
3 tbsp. sugar, 3 tbsp. fish sauce
1/2-3/4 cup hot water, 3 tbsp. cooking oil
lettuce and coriander leaves,
coriander, hot chillies

PREPARATION

1. Clean tapioca pellets. Adding hot water a little at a time, knead until soft and then let stand for an hour. Then form into 1/2 inch balls.

2. Fry coriander root until fragrant. Add pork and fry until done, adding sugar and fish sauce to obtain sweet and salty taste. Add onion and continue frying until dry, then add peanuts and pepper, mix in, and dip out of pan.

3. Flatten out tapioca ball into thin sheet, place 1-1 1/2 tsp. filling on sheet and wrap up to form a secure ball. Line steamer tray with banana leaf or foil, brush with cooking oil and place balls on it, taking care not to crowd balls in tray. Steam 15 minutes, and sprinkle with fried garlic, serve.

4. Serve with fresh vegetables and hot chillies.

เครื่องปรุง

สาคูเม็ดเล็ก 1 1/2 ถ้วย
หมูสับ 1 ถ้วย
หอมใหญ่หั่นเล็ก ๆ 1 ถ้วย
ถั่วลิสงคั่วป่น 1/2 ถ้วย
กระเทียม 4 กลีบ
รากผักชีโขลก 1/2 ช้อนชา
กระเทียมเจียว 3 ช้อนโต๊ะ
พริกไทยป่น 1/4 ช้อนชา
น้ำตาล 3 ช้อนโต๊ะ
น้ำปลา 3 ช้อนโต๊ะ
น้ำร้อน 1/2-3/4 ถ้วย
น้ำมัน 3 ช้อนโต๊ะ
ผักสด : ผักกาดหอม ผักชี พริกขี้หนู

วิธีทำ

1. ฝัดสาคูให้สะอาด ใส่น้ำร้อนทีละน้อย นวดจนนุ่ม หมักทิ้งไว้ 1 ชั่วโมง ปั้นเป็นก้อนกลมเส้นผ่าศูนย์-กลางขนาด 1/2 นิ้ว

2. เจียวรากผักชีกับน้ำมันให้หอม ใส่เนื้อหมู ผัดให้สุก ปรุงรสด้วยน้ำตาล น้ำปลา ใส่หอมใหญ่ ผัดจนแห้ง ใส่ถั่วลิสง พริกไทย ผัดให้เข้ากัน ตักขึ้น

3. แผ่สาคูให้บาง ตักไส้ใส่ 1-1 1/2 ช้อนชา ห่อให้มิด ปูใบตองในลังถึง เรียงสาคูอย่าให้ติดกันมาก นึ่งนาน 15 นาที ยกลง พรมด้วยกระเทียมเจียว

4. จัดใส่จานรับประทานกับผักสดและพริกขี้หนู

TOM SOM PLA TU SOD

Sweet and Sour fresh mackerel soup

ต้มส้มปลาทูสด

INGREDIENTS

5 fresh mackerel or other fish meat

5 spring shallots, cut into 1 inch lengths

3 coriander leaves

1 tbsp. shredded young ginger

5 shallots

1 tbsp. sliced coriander root

7 pepper corns

1 tsp. shrimp paste or anchovy

5 tbsp. palm sugar or sugar

3 tbsp. fish sauce

1/4 cup tamarind juice or lime juice

3 cups water

PREPARATION

1. Cut mackerel's head and wash.

2. Pound together coriander root, pepper, shallots, and shrimp paste until well blended, mix with 3 cups water in a pot, and heat. Add tamarind or lime juice, palm sugar or sugar, and fish sauce. When boiling, add mackerel and shredded ginger.

3. When fish are done, add spring shallots, stir, and remove from heat. Dip into serving bowl, sprinkle with chopped coriander leaves, and serve hot.

เครื่องปรุง

ปลาทูสด 5 ตัว

ต้นหอมหั่นท่อนยาว 1 นิ้ว 5 ต้น

ผักชีเด็ดเป็นใบ 3 ต้น

ขิงอ่อนซอย 1 ช้อนโต๊ะ

หอมแดง 5 หัว

รากผักชีหั่น 1 ช้อนโต๊ะ

พริกไทย 7 เม็ด

กะปิ 1 ช้อนชา

น้ำตาลปีบ 5 ช้อนโต๊ะ

น้ำปลา 3 ช้อนโต๊ะ

น้ำมะขามเปียก 1/4 ถ้วย

น้ำ 3 ถ้วย

วิธีทำ

1. ล้างปลาทู ผ่าท้องควักไส้ออก ตัดหัวออก ล้างให้หมดเมือก

2. โขลกรากผักชี พริกไทย หอมแดง กะปิ เข้าด้วยกันให้ละเอียด ใส่ลงในหม้อ ใส่น้ำ 3 ถ้วย ละลายเข้าด้วยกัน ตั้งไฟ ใส่น้ำมะขามเปียก น้ำตาล น้ำปลา พอเดือด ใส่ปลาทู ขิงซอย

3. เมื่อปลาสุก โรยต้นหอม คนพอทั่ว ยกลง ตักใส่ชาม โรยผักชี เสิร์ฟร้อนๆ

TOM KHLONG
Sour fish soup
ต้มโคล้ง

INGREDIENTS

300 grams dried fish
(or fresh shrimp)
1 cup young tamarind leaves or flowers
(if unavailable, use 2-3 ripe tamarinds)
1 coriander leaves
5 hot chillies
(or 1 dried chilli roasted until fragrant)
5-6 shallots
1 tbsp. salt (or 2-3 tbsp. fish sauce)
3 cups water

PREPARATION

1. Wash fish, roast until fragrant, and cut into small slices.
2. Bring water to a boil, then add crushed shallots and fish. Boil until fish is tender, skimming off broth. Add tamarind flowers and season with tamarind juice (or lemon juice) and salt (or fish sauce) to obtain a sour and salty taste. Add chillies, coriander leaves, and serve hot.

เครื่องปรุง

ปลาแห้ง หรือปลาช่อนแห้ง 300 กรัม
(หรือใช้กุ้งแทนก็ได้)
ใบมะขามอ่อนหรือดอกมะขาม 1 ถ้วย
ผักชีเด็ดเป็นใบ 1 ต้น
พริกขี้หนู 5 เม็ด
(หรือใช้พริกแห้งปิ้งไฟให้หอม 1 เม็ด)
หอมแดง 5-6 หัว
เกลือป่น 1 ช้อนโต๊ะ
(หรือน้ำปลา 2-3 ช้อนโต๊ะ)
น้ำ 3 ถ้วย

วิธีทำ

1. ล้างปลา ปิ้งไฟพอหอม หั่นชิ้นเล็กๆ
2. ใส่น้ำลงในหม้อ พอเดือด ทุบหอมแดงใส่ ใส่ปลา เคี่ยวไฟอ่อนจนเนื้อปลานุ่ม ช้อนฟองออก ใส่ดอก-มะขาม ชิมดูถ้าไม่เปรี้ยวเติมน้ำมะขามเปียกหรือน้ำมะนาว เกลือหรือน้ำปลาให้มีรสจัด เปรี้ยว เค็ม ใส่พริกขี้หนู ผักชี เสิร์ฟร้อนๆ

KAENG JEUT RUAM MID

Chicken, pork, shrimp soup

แกงจืดรวมมิตร

INGREDIENTS

1/2 cup chicken, 1/2 cup pork
1/2 cup shelled shrimp
1 Chinese radish
1 carrot
1/4 tsp. ground pepper
1-2 tbsp. light soy sauce or fish sauce
5 cups soup stock
coriander and spring shallot

PREPARATION

1. Slice chicken and pork into small pieces.
2. Wash and peel the radish and carrot, cut channels down the length, then cut into 1/4 inch thick slices (or carve to look like flowers or leaves)
3. Heat soup stock, add radish and carrot, and cook over low heat until tender, then add the pork, chicken and shrimp, boil and season to taste. When done, add a little sliced spring shallot. Dip into serving bowl, sprinkle with pepper and coriander, and serve immediately.

เครื่องปรุง

เนื้อไก่ เนื้อหมูอย่างละ 1/2 ถ้วย
กุ้งชีแฮ้แกะเปลือกแล้ว 1/2 ถ้วย
หัวไชเท้า 1 หัว
แครอท 1 หัว
พริกไทยป่น 1/4 ช้อนชา
ซีอิ๊วขาวหรือน้ำปลา 1-2 ช้อนโต๊ะ
น้ำซุป 5 ถ้วย
ผักชี ต้นหอม

วิธีทำ

1. หั่นเนื้อไก่ เนื้อหมู เป็นชิ้นเล็กๆ
2. ล้างหัวไชเท้า แครอท ปอกเปลือกแล้วจักเป็น ร่องๆ (หรือทำเป็นรูปดอกไม้ ใบไม้) หั่นหนาประ- มาณ 1/4 นิ้ว
3. ใส่น้ำซุปลงในหม้อ ตั้งไฟ ใส่หัวไชเท้า แครอท ลงต้มไฟอ่อนๆ จนสุก จึงใส่เนื้อหมู ไก่ กุ้ง พอเดือด ปรุงรสด้วยซีอิ๊วขาว ใส่ต้นหอมที่หั่นเป็นท่อนเพียง เล็กน้อย ตักใส่ชาม โรยพริกไทยและผักชี เสิร์ฟทันที

NEUA TUN
Stewed beef
เนื้อตุ๋น

INGREDIENTS	เครื่องปรุง
500 grams beef shank	เนื้อเอ็นน่อง 500 กรัม
200 grams lettuce or swamp cabbage or bean sprouts	ผักกาดหอมหรือผักบุ้งจีน หรือถั่วงอก 200 กรัม
2 Chinese celery plants	ขึ้นฉ่าย 2 ต้น
2 tbsp. fried garlic, 3 coriander roots	กระเทียมเจียว 2 ช้อนโต๊ะ
1/2 inch length of galangal	รากผักชี 3 ราก
1 cm. length of cinnamon	ข่าชิ้นขนาด 1/2 นิ้ว
1 bay leaf	อบเชยชิ้นเล็ก ๆ ขนาด 1 ซม.
2 tsp. salt	ใบกระวาน 1 ใบ
2 tbsp. light soy sauce	เกลือป่น 2 ช้อนชา
1 tbsp. dark soy sauce	ซีอิ๊วขาว 2 ช้อนโต๊ะ
6 cups water	ซีอิ๊วดำ 1 ช้อนโต๊ะ
	น้ำ 6 ถ้วย

PREPARATION

1. Wash meat, cut into large pieces, place in pot. Add water, cinnamon, coriander roots, light soy sauce, dark soy sauce, salt, and bay leaf. Heat to a boil, then cover, reduce heat, and simmer until the meat is tender. (If using an ordinary pot, this will be 3-4 hours.) Season to taste and bring to a boil once again.

2. Blanch only swamp cabbage, other vegetables needn't blanch, cut into 1 inch pieces, and place in bottom of serving bowl. Place stewed beef on the vegetable, sprinkle with coarsely cut celery, fried garlic, and pepper, and serve with rice or noodles.

3. If you like sour taste add 1 tbsp. lime juice.

วิธีทำ

1. ล้างเนื้อหั่นเป็นชิ้นใหญ่ ๆ ใส่หม้อ ใส่น้ำ อบเชย ข่า รากผักชี ซีอิ๊วขาว ซีอิ๊วดำ เกลือ ใบกระวาน ตั้งไฟ พอเดือดลดไฟอ่อน ๆ ปิดฝา เคี่ยวจนเปื่อย (ถ้า เคี่ยวหม้อธรรมดาใช้น้ำ 10 ถ้วย นาน 3-4 ชั่วโมง) ปรุงรส ชิมรส ตั้งไฟให้เดือด

2. ต้มผักบุ้งพอสุก ตักขึ้นหั่นชิ้นสั้น ๆ ขนาด 1 นิ้ว ใส่ชาม ตักเนื้อตุ๋น โรยด้วยขึ้นฉ่ายหั่นหยาบ ๆ กระ- เทียมเจียว พริกไทย รับประทานกับก๋วยเตี๋ยวเส้น- ใหญ่ หรือเส้นหมี่

KAENG LIANG KUNG SOD

Vegetable soup Thai style

แกงเลียงกุ้งสด

INGREDIENTS

200 grams shelled prawns
1 cup of one of the following :
cauliflower, sponge gourd
ivy guard leaves, baby corn
1/2 cub sweet basil leaves

INGREDIENTS SPICE MIXTURE

10 pepper corns
10 shallots
1 tbsp. shrimp paste
1/2 cup dried shrimp or fish
2-3 tbsp. fish sauce
4 cups soup stock or water

PREPARATION

1. Place spice mixture ingredients in a mortar and pound until mixed thoroughly.
2. Add spice mixture to soup stock (or water) in a pot and heat to boiling, stirring to prevent sticking. Do not cover the pot or allow to boil over.
3. Wash the vegetables. Peel the gourd, and cut into 1 1/2 inch strips. Cut the cauliflower and baby corns into bite size.
4. When the water boils, add fish sauce. Add prawns, vegetables and boil. When vegetables are done, taste and add fish sauce or salt as desired, then remove from heat.

เครื่องปรุง

กุ้งแกะเปลือกแล้ว 200 กรัม
ดอกกะหล่ำ บวบเหลี่ยม ผักตำลึง
ข้าวโพดอ่อน อย่างละ 1 ถ้วย
ใบแมงลัก 1/2 ถ้วย

เครื่องปรุงเครื่องแกง

พริกไทย 10 เม็ด
หอมแดง 10 หัว
กะปิ 1 ช้อนโต๊ะ
กุ้งแห้งหรือปลากรอบ 1/2 ถ้วย
น้ำปลา 2-3 ช้อนโต๊ะ
น้ำหรือน้ำซุป 4 ถ้วย

วิธีทำ

1. โขลกเครื่องแกงทั้งหมดเข้าด้วยกันให้ละเอียด
2. ละลายเครื่องแกงกับน้ำซุปหรือน้ำธรรมดาก็ได้ ตั้งไฟให้เดือด คอยคนระวังอย่าปิดฝา กุ้งจะล้นหกออกหมด
3. ผักชนิดต่างๆ ล้างให้สะอาด ถ้าเป็นบวบต้องปอกและหั่นชิ้นขนาด 1 1/2 นิ้ว หั่นดอกกะหล่ำและข้าวโพดอ่อนเป็นชิ้นพอคำ
4. พอน้ำแกงเดือด ใส่น้ำปลา กุ้ง ใส่ผัก พอสุกชิมรสตามชอบ ยกลง

KAENG SOM PHAK BUNG PHIRK SOD KAB PLA

Sour fish spicy soup with swamp cabbage and fish

แกงส้มผักบุ้งพริกสดกับปลา

INGREDIENTS

300 grams fish meat, slice into bite-sized

500 grams swamp cabbage

6 tomatoes, slices in half

3-4 tbsp. fish sauce

2-3 tbsp. lime juice

2 cups water

INGREDIENTS FOR CHILLI PASTE

3 spur chillies

7 shallots

5 cloves garlic

1 tsp. salt

1 tsp. shrimp paste or anchovy

(Instead of this, use 2 tbsp. of kaeng som chilli paste)

PREPARATION

1. Place spice mixture ingredients in mortar and pound until ground and mixed thoroughly.

2. Select young swamp cabbage stems and cut into short pieces.

3. Place water in a pot and heat. When the water boils, stir in the spice mixture and then add the swamp cabbage. When this is cooked, taste and add fish sauce and lime juice so the flavor is sour and salty. Add the tomatoes, and when the soup boils again, add the fish and cover. When the fish is done, remove from heat.

เครื่องปรุง

เนื้อปลา 300 กรัม

ผักบุ้ง 500 กรัม

มะเขือเทศผ่าครึ่ง 6 ลูก

น้ำปลา 3-4 ช้อนโต๊ะ

น้ำมะนาว 2-3 ช้อนโต๊ะ

น้ำ 2 ถ้วย

เครื่องปรุงเครื่องแกง

พริกชี้ฟ้าสด 3 เม็ด

หอมแดง 7 หัว

กระเทียม 5 กลีบ

เกลือป่น 1 ช้อนชา

กะปิ 1 ช้อนชา

(หรือใช้น้ำพริกแกงส้ม 2 ช้อนโต๊ะ)

วิธีทำ

1. โขลกเครื่องแกงทั้งหมดเข้าด้วยกันให้ละเอียด

2. เลือกผักบุ้ง ใช้ก้านอ่อน ล้างน้ำ หั่นท่อนสั้น

3. ใส่น้ำลงในหม้อ ต้มให้เดือด ละลายเครื่องแกง ใส่ผักบุ้ง ต้มจนผักบุ้งสุกนุ่ม ปรุงรสด้วยน้ำมะนาว น้ำปลา ให้มีรสเปรี้ยว เค็ม ใส่มะเขือเทศ พอเดือด ใส่ปลา ปิดฝา ปลาสุก ยกลง

KAENG KHUA KUNG KAB SAPPHAROD

Pineapple curry with prawns

แกงคั่วกุ้งกับสับปะรด

INGREDIENTS

300 grams shelled white prawns
2 tbsp. kaeng khua chilli paste (See p. 9)
3 cups coconut milk
2 cups coarsely chopped sour pineapple
2 kaffir lime leaves, torn into pieces
2 tbsp. sugar
2 tbsp. tamarind or lime juice
2 tbsp. fish sauce

PREPARATION

1. Skim 3 tbsp. of cream from the coconut milk, heat in a wok. When the oil surfaces, add the pounded chilli paste and stir fry. When fragrant, put in the prawns and pineapple and coconut milk and stir.
2. Season with the tamarind or lime juice, sugar, and fish sauce, add the kaffir lime leaves, and when the curry is boiling once again, remove from the heat.

เครื่องปรุง

กุ้งชีแฮ้ปอกเปลือก 300 กรัม
น้ำพริกแกงคั่ว (ดูหน้า 9) 2 ช้อนโต๊ะ
กะทิ 3 ถ้วย
สับปะรดสับหยาบ ๆ (เลือกชนิดเปรี้ยว) 2 ถ้วย
ใบมะกรูดฉีก 2 ใบ
น้ำตาล 2 ช้อนโต๊ะ
น้ำมะขามเปียก 2 ช้อนโต๊ะ
น้ำปลา 2 ช้อนโต๊ะ

วิธีทำ

1. ช้อนหัวกะทิใส่ลงในกระทะ 3 ช้อนโต๊ะ ตั้งไฟพอแตกมัน ใส่น้ำพริกแกงคั่วลงผัดพอหอม ใส่กุ้ง สับ-ปะรด กะทิที่เหลือทั้งหมด คนให้ทั่ว
2. ปรุงรสด้วยน้ำมะขามเปียก น้ำตาล น้ำปลา ใส่ใบ-มะกรูด พอเดือดทั่ว ยกลง

KAENG KA-RI KAI RUE NEUA

Chicken or beef curry

แกงกะหรี่ไก่หรือเนื้อ

INGREDIENTS

500 grams chicken or beef

2 tbsp. kaeng ka-ri chilli paste (See p. 9)

3 peeled and boiled small potatoes

3 cups coconut milk

2 tbsp. fried shallots

1 tsp. salt

PREPARATION

1. Cut meat 2 inch thick slices.
2. Fry the spice mixture in 2 tbsp. of the oil used for frying the shallots adding the coconut cream in small amounts. Then add the chicken (or beef) and cook with stirring. Spoon into a pot. Add the coconut milk, and salt. Cook the meat until it is tender, add the potatoes.
3. Remove from heat when done, dip into serving bowl, and sprinkle with fried shallots. Serve with cucumber relish.

CUCUMBER RELISH

1. Mix the 1/3 cup vinegar, 2 tsp. sugar, and 1 tsp. salt in a pot, bring to a boil, strain, and allow to cool.
2. Slice the 4 cucumbers, 2 shallots, and 1 red spur chilli just before serving and add the vinegar mixture.

เครื่องปรุง

เนื้อไก่หรือเนื้อวัว 500 กรัม

น้ำพริกแกงกะหรี่ (ดูหน้า 9) 2 ช้อนโต๊ะ

มันฝรั่งหัวเล็กต้ม 3 หัว

กะทิ 3 ถ้วย

หอมแดงเจียว 2 ช้อนโต๊ะ

เกลือป่น 1 ช้อนชา

วิธีทำ

1. หั่นเนื้อไก่หรือเนื้อวัวเป็นชิ้นขนาด 2x2 นิ้ว
2. ผัดน้ำพริกแกงกะหรี่กับน้ำมันที่เจียวหอมแดง 2 ช้อนโต๊ะ ค่อย ๆเติมหัวกะทิ 1 ถ้วย ผัดจนหอม ใส่เนื้อไก่ลงผัด ตักใส่หม้อ เติมกะทิ ปรุงรสให้มีรสเค็มรสเดียว ถ้าจืดเติมเกลือ เคี่ยวจนเนื้อไก่นุ่ม ใส่มันฝรั่งพอสุกนุ่ม ยกลง
3. จัดเสิร์ฟ โรยด้วยหอมเจียว เสิร์ฟกับอาจาดหรือแตงดอง ขิงดอง

เครื่องปรุงอาจาด

แตงกวา 4 ลูก

พริกชี้ฟ้าแดง 1 เม็ด

หอมแดง 2 หัว

น้ำตาลทราย 2 ช้อนชา

เกลือป่น 1 ช้อนชา

น้ำส้มสายชู 1/3 ถ้วย

วิธีทำ

1. ผสมน้ำส้มสายชู น้ำตาล เกลือ ตั้งไฟให้เดือด ยกลงกรอง ทิ้งไว้ให้เย็น
2. หั่นแตงกวา พริกชี้ฟ้าแดง หอมแดง เมื่อจะเสิร์ฟจึงใส่น้ำส้มที่ทำไว้ (ส่วนผสมข้อ 1)

KAENG MATSAMAN NEUA

Beef matsaman curry

แกงมัสมั่นเนื้อ

INGERDIENTS

500 grams. beef

3 tbsp. matsaman chilli paste (See p. 9)

3 cups coconut milk

5 peeled small onions (100 grams)

5 small potatoes (100 grams) peeled and boiled

2 tbsp. roasted peanuts

3 bay leaves

5 roasted cardamom fruits

1 piece of roasted cinnamon, 1 cm. long

3 tbsp. sugar

3 tbsp. tamarind juice or 2 tbsp. lime juice

3 tbsp. lime juice, 3 tbsp. fish sauce

PREPARATION

1. Cut beef into 2 inch chunks.

2. Skim off 1 cup coconut cream to be used in cooking spice mixture. Place the remaining coconut milk in a pot with the chicken, pork, or beef and simmer until tender.

3. Heat coconut cream in a frying pan until oil appears on surface, then add the spice mixture and cook until fragrant. Spoon into the pot with the meat and add the peanuts. Taste and adjust the flavor so it is sweet, salty, and sour by adding tamarind juice, sugar, fish sauce, and lime juice. Add bay leaves, cardamon, cinnamon, potatoes, and onion and simmer until tender.

4. Serve with salted egg,

เครื่องปรุง

เนื้อวัว 500 กรัม

น้ำพริกแกงมัสมั่น (ดูหน้า 9) 3 ช้อนโต๊ะ

กะทิ 3 ถ้วย

หอมใหญ่ (100 กรัม) 5 หัว

มันฝรั่งหัวเล็กต้มสุกปอกเปลือก (100 กรัม) 5 หัว

ถั่วลิสงคั่ว 2 ช้อนโต๊ะ

ใบกระวาน 3 ใบ

ลูกกระวานคั่ว 5 ลูก

อบเชยเผาไฟ ยาวขนาด 1 ซม. 1 แท่ง

น้ำตาล 3 ช้อนโต๊ะ

น้ำมะขามเปียก 3 ช้อนโต๊ะ

น้ำมะนาวหรือน้ำส้มซ่า 3 ช้อนโต๊ะ

น้ำปลา 3 ช้อนโต๊ะ

วิธีทำ

1. หั่นเนื้อวัว ขนาด 2x2 นิ้ว

2. ช้อนหัวกะทิไว้ 1 ถ้วย ไว้สำหรับผัดเครื่องแกง ส่วนกะทิที่เหลือไว้สำหรับเคี่ยวเนื้อ

3. เคี่ยวหัวกะทิให้แตกมัน ใส่น้ำพริกแกงมัสมั่นผัด ให้หอม ตักใส่ในหม้อเนื้อ ใส่ถั่วลิสง ปรุงรสด้วยน้ำ-มะขามเปียก น้ำตาล น้ำมะนาว น้ำปลา ให้ได้สามรส ใส่ใบกระวาน ลูกกระวาน อบเชย มันฝรั่ง หอมใหญ่ ชิมรส เคี่ยวต่อไปจนเนื้อนุ่ม ยกลง

4. จัดเสิร์ฟกับไข่เค็ม

KAENG KHIAO WAN KAI

Chicken green curry

แกงเขียวหวานไก่

INGREDIENTS

300 grams chicken

3 tbsp. kaeng khiao wan chilli paste

(See p. 9)

1/2 cup eggplant, cut into bite-sized or

sweet peas

1 cup coconut cream

1 1/2 cup coconut milk

1/4 cup sweet basil

2 kaffir lime leaves (optional)

1 tbsp. sugar

1 1/2-2 tbsp. fish sauce

1 tbsp. cooking oil

1 shreded red spur chilli for garnish

PREPARATION

1. Cut chicken into long, thin slices, mix 1/2 tsp. salt, and fry until dry.

2. Fry chilli paste with oil until fragrant, reduce heat, add coconut cream a little at a time, and cook with stirring until coconut cream begins to have an oily sheen.

3. Add the chicken and torn kaffir lime leaves and cook a short time, then dip curry into a pot, add the coconut milk and the sugar and fish sauce, and heat. When boiling, add the eggplant or peas. When the meat is done, add the sweet basil and remove from heat. Garnish with chilli.

เครื่องปรุง

เนื้อไก่ 300 กรัม

น้ำพริกแกงเขียวหวาน (ดูหน้า 9) 3 ช้อนโต๊ะ

มะเขือพวง 1/2 ถ้วย

หัวกะทิ 1 ถ้วย

หางกะทิ 1 1/2 ถ้วย

ใบโหระพา 1/4 ถ้วย

ใบมะกรูด 2 ใบ

น้ำตาล 1 ช้อนโต๊ะ

น้ำปลา 1 1/2-2 ช้อนโต๊ะ

น้ำมัน 1 ช้อนโต๊ะ

พริกชี้ฟ้าแดงซอย 1 เม็ด

วิธีทำ

1. หั่นเนื้อไก่เป็นชิ้นเล็กๆ ตามยาว ใส่เกลือ 1/2 ช้อนชา ใส่กระทะรวนให้แห้ง

2. ผัดน้ำพริกแกงเขียวหวานกับน้ำมันให้หอม ตัก หัวกะทิใส่ ใช้ไฟอ่อน ผัดให้แตกมันเล็กน้อย

3. ใส่เนื้อไก่ลงผัด ฉีกใบมะกรูดใส่ แล้วตักใส่หม้อ เติมน้ำกะทิที่เหลือ ปรุงรสด้วยน้ำปลา น้ำตาล พอ เดือด ใส่มะเขือพวง สุกแล้วใส่ใบโหระพา พริกชี้- ฟ้าแดง ยกลง

KAENG PHED PED YANG

Roasted Duck red curry

แกงเผ็ดเป็ดย่าง

INGREDIENTS

1 roasted duck, deboned and
cut into 1 inch strips

2 1/2 cups coconut milk

10 cherry tomatoes

1 cup eggplant, cut into bite-sized
or sweet peas

6 rambutans or pineapple, cut into bite-sized

4 kaffir lime leaves,
torn into pieces (optional)

1 tsp. sugar

1/2 tsp. salt

2 tbsp. fish sauce

1/2 cup water (or chicken stock)

1 1/2 tbsp. cooking oil

3 tbsp. red curry paste (See p. 9)

PREPARATION

1. Put vegetable oil into wok over medium heat and add the red curry paste, stir well, add 3/4 cups coconut milk and stir to mix thoroughly.

2. Add the duck and stir well. Next pour the mixture into a pot, add the remaining coconut milk, water, tomatoes, rambutans or pineapple, eggplants or peas, kaffir lime leaves, sugar, salt and fish sauce. Bring to a boil and remove from heat.

เครื่องปรุง

เป็ดย่างถอดกระดูกออก

หั่นเป็นชิ้นขนาด 1 นิ้ว 1 ตัว

กะทิ 2 1/2 ถ้วย

มะเขือเทศสีดา 10 ผล

มะเขือพวง 1 ถ้วย

เงาะ 6 ผล

ใบมะกรูดฉีก 4 ใบ

น้ำตาลทราย 1 ช้อนชา

เกลือป่น 1/2 ช้อนชา

น้ำปลา 2 ช้อนโต๊ะ

น้ำต้มกระดูกไก่หรือน้ำ 1/2 ถ้วย

น้ำมัน 1 1/2 ช้อนโต๊ะ

น้ำพริกแกงแดง (ดูหน้า 9) 3 ช้อนโต๊ะ

วิธีทำ

1. ผัดน้ำพริกแกงแดงกับน้ำมัน ใช้ไฟกลาง จนหอม ใส่กะทิ 3/4 ถ้วย ผัดให้เข้ากัน

2. ใส่เนื้อเป็ดลงไปผัด ตักส่วนผสมลงในหม้อ เติม กะทิที่เหลือ น้ำต้มกระดูกไก่ ใส่มะเขือเทศ มะเขือ- พวง เงาะ ใบมะกรูด ปรุงรสด้วยน้ำปลา น้ำตาล เกลือ ตั้งไฟต่อจนเดือด ยกลง

KAENG KHUA FAK KAB KAI

Chicken and wax gourd curry

แกงคั่วฟักกับไก่

INGREDIENTS	เครื่องปรุง
300 grams chicken	เนื้อไก่ 300 กรัม
2 tbsp. kaeng khua chilli paste (See p. 9)	น้ำพริกแกงคั่ว (ดูหน้า 9) 2 ช้อนโต๊ะ
500 grams wax gourd	ฟักเขียว 500 กรัม
3 cups coocnut milk	กะทิ 3 ถ้วย
1 thinly sliced red spur chilli	พริกชี้ฟ้าแดงหั่นฝอย 1 เม็ด
2-3 kaffir lime leaves, torn into pieces	ใบมะกรูดฉีก 2-3 ใบ
3 tbsp. sugar	น้ำตาล 3 ช้อนโต๊ะ
3 tbsp. tamarind juice or lime juice	น้ำมะขามเปียกหรือน้ำมะนาว 3 ช้อนโต๊ะ
3 tbsp. fish sauce	น้ำปลา 3 ช้อนโต๊ะ

PREPARATION

1. Clean the chicken, cut into 1 inch pieces, mix with 1 tsp. salt, and fry until dry.

2. Peel gourd, remove seeds, and cut into 1 inch chunks.

3. Skim off 1 cup coconut cream, place in frying pan and heat. When oil begins to appear on surface, add the spice mixture and stir, then add the chicken and cook. Spoon into a pot, add the remaining coconut milk and the wax gourd and heat. When the wax gourd is done, taste and season with tamarind or lime juice, sugar, and fish sauce. Add kaffir lime leaves, red spur chilli and remove from heat.

วิธีทำ

1. ล้างเนื้อไก่ หั่นชิ้นขนาด 1 นิ้ว ใส่เกลือ 1 ช้อนชา ผัดให้แห้ง

2. ปอกเปลือกฟักเอาไส้ออก หั่นชิ้นสี่เหลี่ยมขนาด 1 นิ้ว

3. ช้อนหัวกะทิ 1 ถ้วย ใส่กระทะเคี่ยวให้แตกมันเล็กน้อย ใส่น้ำพริกแกงคั่วลงผัดให้หอม ใส่เนื้อไก่ลงผัด ตักใส่หม้อ ใส่กะทิที่เหลือ ใส่ฟัก ตั้งไฟ พอฟักจวนสุก ปรุงรสด้วยน้ำมะขามเปียก น้ำตาล น้ำปลา ให้ได้ 3 รส ใส่ใบมะกรูด พริกชี้ฟ้าแดง ยกลง

PHA-NAENG NEUA

Beef curried in sweet peanut sauce

พะแนงเนื้อ

INGREDIENTS

400 grams beef, cut into thin strips

2 cups coconut milk

1 thinly sliced red spur chilli

1/2 cup ground roasted peanuts

6 kaffir lime leaves, torn into pieces

3 tbsp. sugar

1/4 tsp. salt

2 1/2 tbsp. fish sauce

1/4 cup sweet basil

3 tbsp. pha-naeng curry paste

(or red curry paste) (See p. 9)

PREPARATION

1. Put 1 cup coconut milk over medium heat until some of the oil surfaces, add the curry paste and slowly bring to a boil, stirring constantly.

2. Put in beef strips and cook for 5 minutes, add 1 cup coconut milk.

3. Meanwhile, in a bowl, mix the rest of the ingredients except for the kaffir lime leaves. Add this to the curried beef, stir well and simmer about 15 minutes. Add the kaffir lime leaves, sweet basil and remove from the heat.

เครื่องปรุง

เนื้อวัวหั่นเป็นชิ้นยาวบาง 400 กรัม

กะทิ 2 ถ้วย

พริกชี้ฟ้าแดงหั่นฝอย 1 เม็ด

ถั่วลิสงคั่วป่น 1/2 ถ้วย

ใบมะกรูดฉีก 6 ใบ

น้ำตาล 3 ช้อนโต๊ะ

เกลือป่น 1/4 ช้อนชา

น้ำปลา 2 1/2 ช้อนโต๊ะ

ใบโหระพา 1/4 ถ้วย

น้ำพริกแกงพะแนง

หรือแกงแดง (ดูหน้า 9) 3 ช้อนโต๊ะ

วิธีทำ

1. ตั้งกะทิ 1 ถ้วยบนไฟปานกลาง เคี่ยวจนแตกมัน ใส่น้ำพริกพะแนง หมั่นคน ตั้งเคี่ยวจนเป็นสีแดง

2. ใส่เนื้อวัวตั้งไฟต่อ 5 นาที จึงใส่กะทิที่เหลือ

3. ผสมเครื่องปรุงอื่นๆที่เหลือ ยกเว้นใบมะกรูด ลง ในหม้อ คนให้เข้ากัน เคี่ยวต่ออีก 15 นาที ใส่ใบ- มะกรูด ใบโหระพา พริกชี้ฟ้าแดง ยกลง

HOR MOK MU, KAI, OR PLA

Steamed pork, fish, chicken curry

ห่อหมก หมู ไก่ หรือปลา

INGREDIENTS

300 grams pork, chicken, or fish
1 egg, 3 cups coconut milk
2 tbsp. coriander leaves
1 thinly sliced red spur chilli
1/4 cup sweet basil leaves or sliced cabbage
2 kaffir lime leaves, chopped,
3 tbsp. fish sauce
2 tbsp. red curry paste (See p. 9)

PREPARATION

1. Prepare 15 banana leaf cups 2 1/2 inches in diameter, or just cups.
2. If using pork, chop, but not too finely. If chicken, cut into small pieces. If fish, cut into thin slices. If featherback fish is used, scrape flesh from fish and knead in 1 tbsp. finely ground coriander root and pepper. Marinate whichever meat with 1 tbsp. fish sauce.
3. Mix 3/4 cup coconut cream from the top of coconut milk with 1 tsp. rice flour heat to boiling, remove from heat, to be used to top the hor mok.
4. Mix the remaining coconut milk with the spice mixture, then stir in the meat, next the egg, the fish sauce, and then the rest of the coconut milk a little at a time. Finally stir in a little each of sweet basil, coriander, and kaffir lime leaves to add fragrance.
5. Line the bottoms of the banana leaf cups or cups with the remaining sweet basil leaves, fill each cup with the meat mixture, and steam for 15 minutes. Then remove steamer trays, pour some coconut cream onto each hor mok, sprinkle each with coriander, kaffir lime leaves, and red spur chilli, steam for another minute, then remove from steamer.

เครื่องปรุง

เนื้อหมู หรือไก่ หรือปลา 300 กรัม
ไข่ไก่ 1 ฟอง
กะทิ 3 ถ้วย
ผักชีเด็ดเป็นใบ 2 ช้อนโต๊ะ
พริกชี้ฟ้าแดงหั่นฝอย 1 เม็ด
โหระพาเด็ดเป็นใบ
หรือกะหล่ำปลีหั่นฝอย 1/4 ถ้วย
ใบมะกรูดหั่นฝอย 2 ใบ
น้ำปลา 3 ช้อนโต๊ะ
น้ำพริกแกงแดง (ดูหน้า 9) 2 ช้อนโต๊ะ

วิธีทำ

1. สิ่งที่ต้องเตรียม กระทงใบตองเส้นผ่าศูนย์กลาง 2 1/2 นิ้ว 15 กระทง
2. สับเนื้อหมูไม่ต้องละเอียดมาก ถ้าใช้เนื้อไก่ หั่นเป็นชิ้นเล็ก ถ้าใช้ปลา แล่เนื้อหั่นบางๆ ถ้าใช้ปลากรายขูดนวดกับรากผักชี พริกไทย โขลกละเอียด 1 ช้อนโต๊ะ หมักเนื้อสัตว์กับน้ำปลา 1 ช้อนโต๊ะ
3. แบ่งหัวกะทิ 3/4 ถ้วย ใส่แป้งข้าวเจ้า 1 ช้อนชา ตั้งไฟ คนพอเดือด ยกลง เก็บไว้สำหรับหยอดหน้า
4. ละลายหัวกะทิที่เหลือกับน้ำพริก คนให้เข้ากัน ใส่เนื้อหมู คนต่อไป ใส่ไข่ น้ำปลา ใบโหระพา ผักชี ใบมะกรูดเล็กน้อย คนเข้าด้วยกัน จะทำให้มีกลิ่นหอม
5. ใส่ใบโหระพาที่เหลือรองก้นกระทง ตักส่วนผสมใส่ให้เต็มกระทง นึ่งในน้ำเดือด ไฟแรง 15 นาที ยกลง หยอดหน้ากะทิ โรยผักชี ใบมะกรูด พริกชี้ฟ้าแดง นึ่งต่ออีก 1 นาที ยกลง

46

MU REU KAI PHAD KHING SOD

Pork or Chicken stir-fried with fresh ginger

หมูหรือไก่ผัดขิงสด

INGREDIENTS

200 grams thinly sliced pork loin

(or chicken breast)

1 onion

1/2 cup shredded young ginger

6-7 ear mushrooms

1 tomato

3 spring shallots

1 red spur chilli

2 green spur chillies

1 tsp. sugar

2 tsp. fish sauce

1/4 cup cooking oil

PREPARATION

1. Peel the skin from the onion and cut into slices about 1/4 centimeter thick.

2. Cut the basal portion from the ear mushrooms, wash, soak in warm water until softened, and then chop coarsely.

3. Wash the spur chillies and slice diagonally. Wash the tomato, cut it into one-centimeter-thick slices and remove the seeds.

4. Wash the spring shallots and cut them into short sections.

5. Heat the oil into a wok. When hot, put in the onions and then the pork and stir fry.

6. Add the mushrooms, the ginger and the chillies, and season with the fish sauce and sugar, then, add the spring shallots and tomato, stir everything, dip onto platter, and serve with rice.

เครื่องปรุง

เนื้อหมูสันนอกหั่นชิ้นบาง ๆ (หรืออกไก่) 200 กรัม

หอมใหญ่ 1 หัว

ขิงอ่อนหั่นฝอย 1/2 ถ้วย

เห็ดหูหนู 6-7 ดอก

มะเขือเทศ 1 ลูก

ต้นหอม 3 ต้น

พริกชี้ฟ้าแดง 1 เม็ด

พริกชี้ฟ้าเขียว 2 เม็ด

น้ำตาลทราย 1 ช้อนชา

น้ำปลา 2 ช้อนชา

น้ำมัน 1/4 ถ้วย

วิธีทำ

1. ปอกเปลือกหอมใหญ่หั่นเป็นเสี้ยวหนา 1/4 ซม.

2. ตัดรากเห็ดหูหนูออก ล้างให้สะอาด จึงนำไปแช่น้ำร้อนพอนุ่ม หั่นหยาบ ๆ

3. ล้างพริกชี้ฟ้าหั่นแฉลบ ล้างมะเขือเทศและต้นหอม หั่นมะเขือเทศเป็นเสี้ยวหนา 1 ซม. เอาเมล็ดออก

4. หั่นต้นหอมเป็นท่อนสั้น ๆ

5. ใส่น้ำมันลงในกระทะ ตั้งไฟพอร้อน ใส่หอมใหญ่ เนื้อหมู

6. ใส่เห็ดหูหนู ขิง พริกชี้ฟ้า ปรุงรสด้วยน้ำปลา น้ำตาล ใส่ต้นหอม มะเขือเทศ ผัดให้ทั่ว ตักใส่จาน เสิร์ฟกับข้าว

MU PHAD PHRIK SOD

Pork stir-fried with fresh chilli

หมูผัดพริกสด

INGREDIENTS

300 grams thinly sliced pork loin

1 onion

2 red and 2 green spur chillies

1 tsp. sugar

2 tsp. fish sauce

3 tbsp. cooking oil

PREPARATION

1. Wash the chillies and cut diagonally into thin slices. Peel the onion and cut into 1/2 centimeter-thick slices.

2. Heat the oil in a wok. When hot, fry the garlic until fragrant; then, put in the pork and stir fry.

3. When the pork is nearly done, add the chilli and the onion and season with the fish sauce and sugar. Stir everything together, and when the pork is done, dip up onto a platter and serve with hot rice.

เครื่องปรุง

เนื้อหมูสันในหั่นชิ้นบาง 300 กรัม

หอมใหญ่ 1 หัว

พริกชี้ฟ้าเขียวแดงอย่างละ 2 เม็ด

กระเทียมสับ 1 ช้อนชา

น้ำตาลทราย 1 ช้อนชา

น้ำปลา 2 ช้อนชา

น้ำมัน 3 ช้อนโต๊ะ

วิธีทำ

1. ล้างพริกชี้ฟ้าหั่นแฉลบบางๆ ปอกเปลือกหอม-ใหญ่หั่นเป็นเสี้ยวหนา 1/2 ซม.

2. ใส่น้ำมันลงในกระทะ ใส่กระเทียมเจียวพอหอม ใส่เนื้อหมู ผัดพอหมูจวนสุก

3. ใส่พริกชี้ฟ้าเขียวแดง หอมใหญ่ ปรุงรสด้วยน้ำ-ปลา น้ำตาล ผัดพอทั่วจนสุก ตักใส่จาน เสิร์ฟกับข้าวร้อนๆ

PHAD PHRIK KHING MU KAB THUA FAK YAO
Pork fried with, chilli paste, and string beans
ผัดพริกขิงหมูกับถั่วฝักยาว

INGREDIENTS

300 grams pork
200 grams string bean
1/2 tsp. kaffir lime leaves, minced
1 thinly sliced red spur chilli
1 tbsp. sugar
1 tbsp. fish sauce, 2 tbsp. cooking oil

INGREDIENTS FOR CHILLI PASTE

3 dried chillies seeds removed
and soaked in water
7 shallots, 2 garlic bulbs
1 tsp. minced galangal
1 tbsp. finely sliced lemon grass
1 tsp. finely sliced kaffir lime rind
1 tsp. finely sliced coriander root
5 pepper corns, 2 tbsp. ground dried shrimp
1 tsp. salt, 1 tsp. shrimp paste
or 3 tbsp. red curry mixed
2 tbsp. dried shrimps

PREPARATION

1. Place chilli paste ingredients in mortar and pound until thoroughly ground.
2. Wash pork, cut into long, thin slices, and marinate in 1 tsp. fish sauce.
3. Cut beans, into 1 inch, lengths, boil until just cooked, and remove from water.
4. Heat oil in a frying pan, fry the pork until done, then remove the pork from the pan and set aside.
5. Put the spice mixture chilli paste in the pan and fry until fragrant, then add the pork, sugar, fish sauce, and string beans. Stir to mix. When done, scoop up onto serving plate.

เครื่องปรุง

เนื้อหมู 300 กรัม ถั่วฝักยาว 200 กรัม
ใบมะกรูดหั่นฝอย 1/2 ช้อนชา
พริกชี้ฟ้าแดงหั่นฝอย 1 เม็ด
น้ำตาล 1 ช้อนโต๊ะ น้ำปลา 1 ช้อนโต๊ะ
น้ำมัน 2 ช้อนโต๊ะ

เครื่องปรุงเครื่องแกง

พริกแห้งแกะเมล็ดออกแช่น้ำ 3 เม็ด
หอมแดง 7 หัว
กระเทียม 2 หัว
ข่าหั่นละเอียด 1 ช้อนชา
ตะไคร้หั่นละเอียด 1 ช้อนโต๊ะ
ผิวมะกรูดหั่นละเอียด 1 ช้อนชา
รากผักชีหั่นละเอียด 1 ช้อนชา
พริกไทย 5 เม็ด
กุ้งแห้งป่น 2 ช้อนโต๊ะ
เกลือป่น 1 ช้อนชา
กะปิ 1 ช้อนชา หรือน้ำพริกแกงแดง 3 ช้อนโต๊ะ
ผสมกับกุ้งแห้งป่น 2 ช้อนโต๊ะ

วิธีทำ

1. โขลกเครื่องแกงทั้งหมดเข้าด้วยกันให้ละเอียด
2. ล้างเนื้อหมู หั่นชิ้นเล็ก ๆ ยาว ๆ หมักกับน้ำปลา 1 ช้อนชา
3. ล้างถั่วฝักยาว ตัดเป็นท่อนยาว 1 นิ้ว ต้มพอสุก ตักขึ้น
4. ใส่น้ำมันลงในกระทะ ผัดเนื้อหมู พอสุก ตักขึ้น
5. ใส่เครื่องแกงลงผัดให้หอม จึงใส่เนื้อหมูลงผัด ปรุงรสด้วยน้ำตาล น้ำปลา ใส่ถั่วฝักยาว ผัดพอสุกทั่ว ตักใส่จาน เสิร์ฟ

PHAD KHI MAO KUNG

Spicy stir-fried prawns

ผัดขี้เมากุ้ง

INGREDIENTS
500 grams tiger prawns
1/4 cup holy basil tips
1 tsp. sugar
2 tbsp. fish sauce
3 tbsp. cooking oil

INGREDIENTS FOR CHILLI PASTE
6 yellow spur chillies
5 shallots
10 garlic cloves
1/2 tsp. shrimp paste

PREPARATION

1. Pound the spice mixture ingredients just enough to mix them together.
2. Shell the prawns, but leave the tail fins attached, remove the heads.
3. Wash the basil.
4. Put the oil into a wok over medium heat, add the chilli paste, and stir fry until fragrant; then, add the prawns and continue stir frying until they are done. Season with the fish sauce and sugar, mix everything together well, add the basil, stir to mix, and then dip out onto a serving platter.

เครื่องปรุง
กุ้งกุลาดำ 500 กรัม
กะเพราเด็ดเป็นใบ 1/4 ถ้วย
น้ำตาลทราย 1 ช้อนชา
น้ำปลา 2 ช้อนโต๊ะ
น้ำมัน 3 ช้อนโต๊ะ

เครื่องปรุงเครื่องแกง
พริกชี้ฟ้าเหลือง 6 เม็ด
หอมแดง 5 หัว
กระเทียม 10 กลีบ
กะปิ 1/2 ช้อนชา

วิธีทำ

1. โขลกเครื่องแกงทั้งหมดเข้าด้วยกัน ไม่ต้องละ-เอียดมาก
2. แกะเปลือกกุ้ง เด็ดหัวและหางออก พักไว้
3. ล้างใบกะเพราให้สะอาด
4. ใส่น้ำมันลงในกระทะ ตั้งไฟกลาง ผัดน้ำพริกขี้เมากับน้ำมันจนหอม ใส่กุ้ง พอกุ้งสุก ปรุงรสด้วยน้ำปลา น้ำตาล ผัดให้เข้ากันอีกครั้ง ใส่ใบกะเพรา ผัดให้ทั่ว ตักใส่จาน เสิร์ฟ

PHAD PHAK RUAM MID

Stir-fried asparagus, carrot, and cauliflower with mushrooms

ผัดผักรวมมิตร

INGREDIENTS	เครื่องปรุง
200 grams rice-straw mushrooms	เห็ดฟาง 200 กรัม
200 grams asparagus	หน่อไม้ฝรั่ง 200 กรัม
1 carrot	แครอท 1 หัว
1 head cauliflower	ดอกกะหล่ำ 1 หัว
2 tsp. coarsely chopped garlic	กระเทียมสับหยาบ 2 ช้อนชา
1 tsp. sugar	น้ำตาลทราย 1 ช้อนชา
2 tsp. fish sauce	น้ำปลา 2 ช้อนชา
3 tbsp. water	น้ำ 3 ช้อนโต๊ะ
3 tbsp. cooking oil	น้ำมัน 3 ช้อนโต๊ะ

PREPARATION

1. Wash the carrot and boil in water until done, then, remove from the water, peel, and cut into disk-shaped slices one centimeter thick.

2. Wash the mushrooms and trim any foreign matter off the stems. Wash the cauliflower and separate the flowerets. Wash the asparagus, trim off a tough portions, and cut into short lengths.

3. Heat the oil in a wok. When hot, fry the garlic until it turns yellow, add the cauliflower. Add the water and then the mushrooms, cook with stirring, add the asparagus and then the carrot.

4. Season with the fish sauce and sugar, stir to mix well, and when everything is done, dip up onto a serving platter.

วิธีทำ

1. ล้างแครอทให้สะอาด นำไปต้มในน้ำเดือดทั้งหัว ต้มพอสุก ปอกเปลือก หั่นแว่นหนา 1 ซม.

2. ล้างเห็ดฟาง เฉือนโคนส่วนที่สกปรกออก ล้าง ดอกกะหล่ำและหน่อไม้ฝรั่ง หั่นดอกกะหล่ำเป็นดอก เล็กๆ หั่นหน่อไม้ฝรั่งเป็นท่อนสั้น (ส่วนที่แก่ปอก เปลือกออก)

3. ใส่น้ำมันลงในกระทะ ใส่กระเทียมเจียวพอเหลือง ใส่ดอกกะหล่ำ น้ำ เห็ดฟาง ผัดพอทั่ว ใส่หน่อไม้ฝรั่ง แครอท

4. ปรุงรสด้วยน้ำปลา น้ำตาล ผัดให้ทั่ว พอสุก ตัก ใส่จาน เสิร์ฟ

PHAD PHED KUNG

Stir-fried prawn with red curry paste

ผัดเผ็ดกุ้ง

INGREDIENTS

200 grams rice-straw mushrooms,
sliced in haft

6 shelled prawns

1/4-1/2 cup eggplant,
cut into bite sized pieces

1 thinly sliced red spur chilli

1/4 cup. green pepper

3 tbsp. sweet basil leaves

2-3 tbsp. red curry paste (See p. 9)

1 tsp. sugar

2 tbsp. fish sauce

1/2 cup water

1/2 cup cooking oil

PREPARATION

1. Heat the oil in a wok. When hot, stir fry the red curry paste until fragrant and then add mushrooms and prawns, cook it until done.

2. Add sugar, fish sauce, water and continue stir fry then add eggplant, green pepper, red spur chilli, sweet basil, and continue stir frying until the eggplant is done.

3. Dip out onto a platter and serve .

เครื่องปรุง

เห็ดฟางผ่าครึ่ง 200 กรัม

กุ้งปอกเปลือก 6 ตัว

มะเขือเปราะผ่าสี่ 1/4-1/2 ถ้วย

พริกชี้ฟ้าแดงหั่นเป็นเส้น 1 เม็ด

พริกไทยอ่อน 1/4 ถ้วย

โหระพาเด็ดเป็นใบ 3 ช้อนโต๊ะ

น้ำพริกแกงเผ็ด (ดูหน้า 9) 2-3 ช้อนโต๊ะ

น้ำตาล 1 ช้อนชา

น้ำปลา 2 ช้อนโต๊ะ

น้ำ 1/2 ถ้วย

น้ำมัน 1/2 ถ้วย

วิธีทำ

1. ใส่น้ำมันลงในกระทะ ตั้งไฟ พอร้อนใส่น้ำพริกแกงเผ็ด ผัดให้หอม ใส่เห็ดฟาง กุ้ง ผัดพอสุก

2. ปรุงรสด้วยน้ำตาล น้ำปลา ใส่น้ำ ผัดให้เข้ากันดี ใส่มะเขือเปราะ เม็ดพริกไทยอ่อน พริกชี้ฟ้าแดง โหระพา ผัดพอทั่ว พอมะเขือสุก ปิดไฟ ตักใส่จาน เสิร์ฟ

PLA KAO RAD PHRIK KAENG

Fried grouper with chilli sauce

ปลาเก๋าราดพริกแกง

INGREDIENTS

1 grouper weighing 300 grams

1 tsp. finely sliced kaffir lime leaves (optinal)

1 sliced red spur chilli

1 tsp. sugar

2 tsp. lime juice

2 cups cooking oil

INGREDIENTS FOR CHILLI PASTE

3 large dried chillies, seeds removed and soaked in water

2 tbsp. sliced shallots

1 tbsp. sliced garlic

1 tsp. minced galangal

1 tbsp. sliced lemon grass

1 tsp. salt

1 tsp. shrimp paste

or 3 tbsp. red curry pastes

PREPARATION

1. Pound the chilli paste ingredients until well ground and thoroughly mixed.

2. Scale and clean the grouper. Wipe dry. Make widely spaced slashes on both sides, and rub with the lime juice.

3. Heat 2 cups of the oil in wok. When hot, fry the fish until golden brown on both sides, and then remove from the oil and drain.

4. Heat the 2 tbsp. of the oil in a wok. When hot, stir fry the chilli paste until fragrant, add the sugar, stir to mix thoroughly, and dip out over the grouper. Garnish with red spur chilli and kaffir lime leaves.

เครื่องปรุง

ปลาเก๋า น้ำหนักประมาณ 300 กรัม 1 ตัว

ใบมะกรูดหั่นฝอย 1 ช้อนชา

พริกชี้ฟ้าแดงหั่นเฉียง 1 เม็ด

น้ำตาลทราย 1 ช้อนชา

น้ำมะนาว 2 ช้อนชา

น้ำมัน 2 ถ้วย

เครื่องปรุงเครื่องแกง

พริกแห้งแกะเมล็ดออกแช่น้ำ 3 เม็ด

หอมแดงซอย 2 ช้อนโต๊ะ

กระเทียมซอย 1 ช้อนโต๊ะ

ข่าหั่นละเอียด 1 ช้อนชา

ตะไคร้ซอย 1 ช้อนโต๊ะ

เกลือป่น 1 ช้อนชา

กะปิ 1 ช้อนชา

หรือน้ำพริกแกงเผ็ด 3 ช้อนโต๊ะ

วิธีทำ

1. โขลกเครื่องแกงทั้งหมดเข้าด้วยกันให้ละเอียด

2. ขอดเกล็ดปลา ผ่าท้องควักไส้ออก ซับให้แห้ง บั้ง ห่างๆ ทั้งสองด้าน ทาด้วยน้ำมะนาวทั้งสองด้าน

3. ใส่น้ำมันลงในกระทะ ตั้งไฟพอน้ำมันร้อน ใส่ปลา ทอดให้เหลือง ตักขึ้นให้สะเด็ดน้ำมัน

4. แบ่งน้ำมันใส่กระทะ 2 ช้อนโต๊ะ ใส่น้ำพริก ผัดให้ หอม ใส่น้ำตาล ผัดให้เข้ากัน ตักราดบนตัวปลา แต่งด้วยพริกชี้ฟ้าแดง และใบมะกรูด เสิร์ฟ

KHAI JIAO MU SAB

Ground pork omelette

ไข่เจียวหมูสับ

INGREDIENTS

3 eggs
1/2 cup ground pork
1 thinly sliced spring shallots
1 finely sliced spur red chilli
1/8 tsp. ground pepper
2 tsp. fish sauce
2 tbsp. water
1/4 cup cooking oil

PREPARATION

1. Break the eggs into a bowl, add the pork, fish sauce, and pepper, spring shallots, and beat to mix thoroughly.
2. Heat the oil in a wok. When hot, pour in half of the egg mixture. When done on one side, turn and fry until done on the other. Fry the remainder of the egg mixture in the same way. Sprinkle with onions and chilli.
3. Serve with hot rice.

เครื่องปรุง

ไข่ไก่ 3 ฟอง
หมูบด 1/2 ถ้วย
ต้นหอมซอย 1 ต้น
พริกชี้ฟ้าแดงหั่นฝอย 1 เม็ด
พริกไทยป่น 1/8 ช้อนชา
น้ำปลา 2 ช้อนชา
น้ำ 2 ช้อนโต๊ะ
น้ำมัน 1/4 ถ้วย

วิธีทำ

1. ต่อยไข่ใส่ถ้วย ใส่หมูบด น้ำปลา พริกไทย ต้นหอม ตีพอเข้ากัน
2. ใส่น้ำมันลงในกระทะ ตั้งไฟพอร้อน แบ่งไข่เป็น 2 ส่วน ใส่ไข่ทอด พอไข่ด้านหนึ่งสุก พลิกกลับทอดอีกด้าน ที่เหลือทอดแบบเดียวกัน
3. โรยด้วยพริกชี้ฟ้าแดง จัดเสิร์ฟกับข้าวร้อน ๆ

THOD MUN PLA
Fried fish cakes
ทอดมันปลา

INGREDIENTS

500 grams white fish meat (e.g.ladyfinger),
minced of chopped

1 egg

1/2 cup string beans, sliced fine

3 tbsp. kaffir lime leaves, minced or chopped

1 tsp. sugar

1 tsp. salt

1 tbsp. red curry paste (See p. 9)

3 cups cooking oil for frying

INGREDIENTS FOR CUCUMBER RELISH

1 cup diced cucumber

1/2 cup ground roasted peanuts

1/2 cup sugar

1/2 cup vinegar

Mix sugar and vinegar in the pot and heat. When the mixture come to boil, remove from the heat and allow to cool, spoon in a cup add diced cucumber top with ground peanuts.

PREPARATION

1. Put all the ingredients in a large bowl and mix well knead, with the hand until it stick.
2. Spoon the mixture 2 tbsp.; shape into small patties about 3 in diameter and deep fry in vegetable oil until golden brown.
3. Serve with cucumber relish.

เครื่องปรุง

เนื้อปลาขูด 500 กรัม

ไข่ไก่ 1 ฟอง

ถั่วฝักยาวหั่นฝอย 1/2 ถ้วย

ใบมะกรูดซอย 3 ช้อนโต๊ะ

น้ำตาลทราย 1 ช้อนชา

เกลือป่น 1 ช้อนชา

น้ำพริกแกงเผ็ด (ดูหน้า 9) 1 ช้อนโต๊ะ

น้ำมันสำหรับทอด 3 ถ้วย

เครื่องปรุงอาจาด

แตงกวาผ่าสี่หั่นหนา 1 ซม. 1 ถ้วย

ถั่วลิสงคั่วโขลกหยาบ ๆ 1/2 ถ้วย

น้ำตาลทราย 1/2 ถ้วย

น้ำส้มสายชู 1/2 ถ้วย

ผสมน้ำตาลและน้ำส้มสายชูเข้าด้วยกัน ตั้งไฟพอน้ำตาลละลาย ทิ้งไว้ให้เย็น ตักใส่ถ้วย ใส่แตง-กวา โรยด้วยถั่วลิสง

วิธีทำ

1. ผสมเครื่องปรุงทั้งหมดเข้าด้วยกัน ใช้มือนวดจนเหนียว
2. ปั้นส่วนผสมเป็นก้อนประมาณ 2 ช้อนโต๊ะ แล้วแผ่เป็นแผ่นกลม เส้นผ่าศูนย์กลางประมาณ 3 นิ้ว ทอดในน้ำมันร้อน ไฟแรงปานกลาง จนสุกเหลืองดี ตักขึ้น พักไว้ให้สะเด็ดน้ำมัน
3. เสิร์ฟกับอาจาด

KAI HO BAI TEUI

Fied chicken in wrapped with pandanus leaf

ไก่ห่อใบเตย

INGREDIENTS

**600 grams (about 3 cups)
bite-sized pieces of chicken breast
2 tsp. garlic, 1/2 tsp. ground pepper
2 tsp. sugar, 2 tbsp. light soy sauce
1 tbsp. sesame oil
30-35 fragrant pandanus leaves or foil
4-5 cups cooking oil for frying**

PREPARATION

1. Place the sliced chicken in a bowl. Pound the garlic and pepper until finely ground, and sprinkle over the chicken. Add the soy sauce, sesame oil, and sugar, gently mix together, and allow to marinate for at least an hour.

2. Wrap the chicken with the pandanus leaf or foil so as to form triangular packets and tie close with banana fiber.

3. Deep fry the packets in hot oil over medium heat. When done, remove from the oil and drain on absorbent paper to soak up as much oil as possible.

4. When served, the chicken is removed from the pandanus wrapper and eaten with a dipping sauce, worcestershire sauce, or chilli sauce.

INGREDIENTS SAUCE

Put the water 2 tbsp. and the sugar 4 tbsp. in a pot, heat until the mixture boils and the sugar has dissolved, and then remove from the heat. Then, add the dark soy sauce, 1 tsp. salt, and roasted 2 tbsp.

เครื่องปรุง

เนื้ออกไก่หั่นเป็นชิ้นพอคำ 600 กรัม
หรือประมาณ 3 ถ้วย กระเทียม 2 ช้อนชา
พริกไทยป่น 1/2 ช้อนชา น้ำตาลทราย 2 ช้อนชา
ซีอิ๊วขาว 2 ช้อนโต๊ะ น้ำมันงา 1 ช้อนโต๊ะ
ใบเตยหอมชนิดใบใหญ่ 30-35 ใบ
น้ำมันสำหรับทอด 4-5 ถ้วย

วิธีทำ

1. โขลกกระเทียม พริกไทย เข้าด้วยกันให้ละเอียด ใส่ในชามไก่ที่หั่นไว้แล้วเคล้าด้วยซีอิ๊วขาว น้ำมันงา น้ำตาล หมักไว้อย่างน้อย 1 ชั่วโมง

2. ห่อไก่ด้วยใบเตย โดยห่อให้เป็นรูปสามเหลี่ยม มัด ด้วยเชือก หรือห่อแบบสอดให้แน่น

3. ทอดในน้ำมันร้อนจัด ไฟปานกลาง พอสุก ตักขึ้น ใส่ตะแกรงให้สะเด็ดน้ำมัน หรือถ้วยกระดาษฟาง สำหรับซับน้ำมันไว้

4. แกะเนื้อไก่ออกจากห่อ รับประทานกับน้ำจิ้มซอส-เปรี้ยวหรือซอสพริกก็ได้

เครื่องปรุงน้ำจิ้ม

น้ำตาลทราย 4 ช้อนโต๊ะ น้ำ 2 ช้อนโต๊ะ
ซีอิ๊วดำ 3 ช้อนโต๊ะ เกลือป่น 1 ช้อนชา
งาขาวคั่วบุบพอแตก 2 ช้อนโต๊ะ

ใส่น้ำ น้ำตาลทราย ลงในหม้อ นำไปตั้งไฟให้ เดือด น้ำตาลละลาย ยกลง ทิ้งให้เย็น ใส่ซีอิ๊วดำ เกลือ งาคั่ว ผสมให้เข้ากัน ชิมรสตามชอบ ถ้าชอบ รสเปรี้ยว จะใส่น้ำส้มสายชูนิดหน่อยก็ได้

sesame seeds and mix. Season additionally as desired. If a sour taste is desired, add a little vinegar.

YAM THALE
Sour and spicy seafood salad
ยำทะเล

INGREDIENTS

200 grams shelled scalded tiger prawns,
heads and tail fins removed
100 grams bite-sized pieces of squid, surfaces
slashed in a cris-cross pattern
100 grams scalded shelled mussels
100 grams scalded fish balls
1/2 cup Chinese celery or celery, cut into
short lengths
1 shallot, cut into thin slices
1 lettuce plant

INGREDIENTS FOR THE DRESSING

2 red spur chillies, pounded well
5 garlic cloves, pounded well
1 tsp. sugar
1/4 cup lime juice
1/4 cup fish sauce

PREPARATION

1. Mix the ingredients for the dressing together.

2. Place the prawns, squid, mussels, fish balls, celery, and shallot in a bowl, add the dressing, and toss gently to mix.

3. Wash the lettuce, cut into pieces, and arrange these on a platter. Spoon the salad onto the lettuce, and serve.

เครื่องปรุง

กุ้งกุลาดำลวกแกะเปลือก
เอาหัวและหางออก 200 กรัม
ปลาหมึกหั่นชิ้นขนาดพอคำบั้งลวก 100 กรัม
หอยแมลงภู่ลวกแกะเอาแต่เนื้อ 100 กรัม
ลูกชิ้นปลาลวก 100 กรัม
ขึ้นฉ่ายหั่นท่อนสั้น 1/2 ถ้วย
หอมแดงหั่นบาง ๆ 1 หัว
ผักกาดหอม 1 ต้น

เครื่องปรุงน้ำยำ

พริกชี้ฟ้าแดงโขลก 2 เม็ด
กระเทียมโขลก 5 กลีบ
น้ำตาลทราย 1 ช้อนชา
น้ำมะนาว 1/4 ถ้วย
น้ำปลา 1/4 ถ้วย

วิธีทำ

1. ผสมเครื่องปรุงน้ำยำเข้าด้วยกัน

2. ใส่กุ้ง ปลาหมึก หอยแมลงภู่ ลูกชิ้นปลา ขึ้นฉ่าย หอมแดง ใส่ลงในชาม ราดด้วยน้ำยำ เคล้าเบา ๆ ให้ทั่ว

3. ล้างผักกาดหอม หั่นเป็นท่อนจัดใส่จาน ตักยำ วางข้างบน เสิร์ฟ

YAM WUN SEN
Spicy mungbean noodle salad
ยำวุ้นเส้น

INGREDIENTS
2 cups short lengths of scalded
mungbean noodles
1/2 cup thin slices of boiled pork
1/2 cup thin slices of boiled pork liver
1/2 cups thin slices of boiled prawn
1/4 cup crisp fried dried shrimp
1/2 cup spring shallots, cut
into short lengths
1/2 cup 1-inch lengths of Chinese celery
1 lettuce plant

INGREDIENTS FOR THE DRESSING
3 hot chillies
1 tsp. thinly sliced bulb of pickled garlic
1 tbsp. thinly sliced coriander root
1/3 cup sugar
1 tsp. salt, 1/3 cup vinegar

Pound the coriander root, pickled garlic, and chilli well in a mortar. Place this mixture in a pot, add the vinegar, sugar and salt, and heat. When the mixture comes to a boil, remove from the heat and allow to cool.

PREPARATION

1. Mix the noodles, pork, liver, prawn, spring shallot, and celery. Add the dressing and toss gently.
2. Place the salad on a bed of lettuce and sprinkle with the fried dried shrimp.

เครื่องปรุง
วุ้นเส้นแช่น้ำหั่นท่อนสั้นลวก 2 ถ้วย
เนื้อหมูต้มหั่นชิ้นบาง 1/2 ถ้วย
ตับหมูต้มหั่นชิ้นบาง 1/2 ถ้วย
กุ้งต้มหั่นชิ้นบาง 1/2 ถ้วย
กุ้งแห้งทอดกรอบ 1/4 ถ้วย
ต้นหอมหั่นท่อนสั้น 1/2 ถ้วย
ขึ้นฉ่ายหั่นท่อนยาว 1 นิ้ว 1/2 ถ้วย
ผักกาดหอมหั่นท่อน 1 นิ้ว 1 ต้น

เครื่องปรุงน้ำยำ
พริกขี้หนู 3 เม็ด
กระเทียมดองหั่นบาง 1 ช้อนชา
รากผักชีหั่นฝอย 1 ช้อนโต๊ะ
น้ำตาลทราย 1/3 ถ้วย
เกลือป่น 1 ช้อนชา
น้ำส้มสายชู 1/3 ถ้วย

โขลกรากผักชีกับกระเทียมดองและพริกขี้หนู พอแหลก ตักใส่หม้อ ใส่น้ำส้มสายชู น้ำตาล และเกลือ ตั้งไฟพอเดือด ยกลง ทิ้งไว้ให้เย็น

วิธีทำ

1. ผสมวุ้นเส้น เนื้อหมู ตับหมู กุ้ง ต้นหอม ขึ้นฉ่าย เข้าด้วยกัน คลุกกับน้ำยำให้ทั่ว
2. ตักเสิร์ฟในจานที่รองด้วยผักกาดหอม โรยหน้า ด้วยกุ้งแห้งทอด

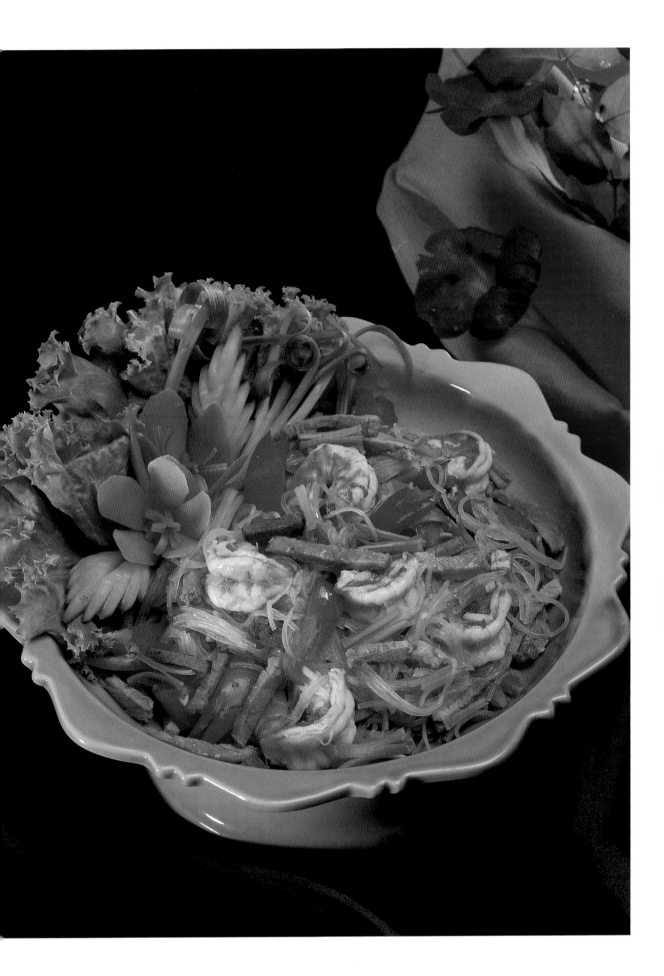

YAM HED FANG

Sour and spicy mushroom salad Thai style

ยำเห็ดฟาง

INGREDIENTS

300 grams rice-straw mushrooms
1/2 cup thinly sliced boiled chicken
1/2 cup thinly sliced boiled prawn
1 onion sliced
1 thinly sliced red spur chilli
2 tbsp. fried shallot

INGREDIENTS FOR THE DRESSING

2 hot chillies
1 tbsp. finely sliced garlic
2 tsp. salt
1/4 cup lime juice

Pound the chillies, garlic, and salt together until finely ground, add the lime juice, and mix thoroughly.

PREPARATION

1. Wash the mushrooms thoroughly and remove any foreign matter from the bases of the stems. Steam over boiling water for about 10 minutes; then, place in a colander and allow to drain.
2. Put the mushrooms in a mixing bowl, add the chicken, prawn, onion, add the dressing, and toss gently to mix thoroughly. Adjust the seasoning.
3. Transfer the salad to a bed of lettuce prepared on a serving platter, sprinkle with the fried shallot and spur chilli, and serve.

เครื่องปรุง

เห็ดฟาง 300 กรัม
เนื้อไก่ต้มหั่นชิ้นเล็กบาง 1/2 ถ้วย
เนื้อกุ้งต้มหั่นบางๆ 1/2 ถ้วย
หอมใหญ่หั่นเสี้ยว 1 หัว
พริกชี้ฟ้าแดงหั่นฝอย 1 เม็ด
หอมแดงเจียว 2 ช้อนโต๊ะ

เครื่องปรุงน้ำยำ

พริกขี้หนู 2 เม็ด
กระเทียมซอย 1 ช้อนโต๊ะ
เกลือป่น 2 ช้อนชา
น้ำมะนาว 1/4 ถ้วย

โขลกพริกขี้หนู กระเทียม เกลือ เข้าด้วยกัน ให้ละเอียด ใส่น้ำมะนาว คนให้เข้ากัน

วิธีทำ

1. ล้างเห็ดฟางให้สะอาด เฉือนโคนที่สกปรกออก ผ่าครึ่ง จัดใส่จาน นำไปนึ่งในน้ำเดือดให้สุก ประมาณ 10 นาที ใส่กระชอน พักไว้ให้สะเด็ดน้ำ
2. ใส่เห็ดฟางในชามผสม ใส่เนื้อไก่ กุ้ง หอมใหญ่ ราดด้วยน้ำยำ เคล้าเบาๆ ให้เข้ากัน ชิมรส
3. ตักใส่จานที่รองด้วยผักกาดหอม โรยหอมแดง-เจียว พริกชี้ฟ้าแดง เสิร์ฟ

YAM NEUA YANG

Barbecued beef salad Thai style

ยำเนื้อย่าง

INGREDIENTS

500 grams (2 cups) round, rump,
or sirloin steak, grilled rare, sliced thin

3-4 lettuce plants

1 mint leaves

10-20 hot chillies

10 garlic cloves

1 tbsp. sugar

3 tbsp. fish sauce

3 tbsp. lemon juice

thinly sliced red spur chillies for garnishing
(alternatively, chillies may be slit part of the
way down the length from the tip, the skin
being curled back to look like flowers).

PREPARATION

1. Mix garlic, hot chillies, fish sauce, lemon juice, and sugar, seasoning to obtain a spicy and toss with meat, onions, and cucumber, place on serving platter, and garnish with coriander and sliced chillies.

2. In another way, arrange the meat, onions, and mint leaves separately on the platter with the chilli saucer in a bowl in the center. The meat, vegetables, and sauce are then mixed at table.

เครื่องปรุง

เนื้อลูกมะพร้าวหรือสะโพก หรือสันในย่างพอสุก
หั่นชิ้นบาง ๆ 500 กรัม

ผักกาดหอม 3-4 ต้น

สะระแหน่เด็ดเป็นใบ 1 ต้น

พริกขี้หนู 10-20 เม็ด

กระเทียม 10 กลีบ

น้ำตาลทราย 1 ช้อนโต๊ะ

น้ำปลา 3 ช้อนโต๊ะ

น้ำมะนาว 3 ช้อนโต๊ะ

พริกชี้ฟ้าแดงหั่นฝอยสำหรับโรยหน้า
หรือจักเป็นดอก

วิธีทำ

1. โขลกกระเทียมกับพริกขี้หนูเข้าด้วยกัน ผสมกับ
น้ำปลา น้ำมะนาว น้ำตาล ชิมรสให้จัดเป็นน้ำยำ

2. คลุกน้ำยำกับเนื้อ สะระแหน่ จัดลงจาน วางพริก-
ชี้ฟ้าแดง หรือจะจัดเนื้อและผักลงในจานเป็นพวก ๆ
ให้ดูงาม วางถ้วยน้ำยำตรงกลางจาน นำไปคลุกที่
โต๊ะอาหารเวลารับประทาน

YAM MA-KHEUA YAO

Savory long eggplant

ยำมะเขือยาว

INGREDIENTS

2 long eggplants

1/4 cup ground pork

3 shelled scalded prawns

2 tbsp. mint leaves

INGREDIENTS FOR THE DRESSTING

2 tsp. sliced hot chilles

3 tbsp. sliced shallot

2-3 tbsp. fish sauce

1/4 cup. lime juice

1 tbsp. sugar

PREPARATON

1. Mix the ingredients for the dressing together.

2. Roast the eggplant over a hot charcoal fire, turning regularly, until soft throughout. Peel the eggplants, and then slice into sections.

3. Add prawn, pork, then add the dressing, and toss gently to mix.

4. Dip out onto a platter, sprinkle with mint leaves and serve.

เครื่องปรุง

มะเขือยาว 2 ลูก

หมูบด 1/4 ถ้วย

กุ้งลวกหั่นชิ้นบาง 3 ตัว

สะระแหน่เด็ดเป็นใบ 2 ช้อนโต๊ะ

เครื่องปรุงน้ำยำ

พริกขี้หนูซอย 2 ช้อนชา

หอมแดงซอย 3 ช้อนโต๊ะ

น้ำปลา 2-3 ช้อนโต๊ะ

น้ำมะนาว 1/4 ถ้วย

น้ำตาลทราย 1 ช้อนโต๊ะ

วิธีทำ

1. ผสมเครื่องปรุงน้ำยำเข้าด้วยกัน

2. ย่างมะเขือให้สุกนุ่ม นำไปปอกเปลือกออก หั่นเป็นท่อนสั้นใส่ชาม

3. ใส่กุ้ง เนื้อหมู ราดด้วยน้ำยำ เคล้าให้ทั่ว

4. ตักใส่จาน โรยสะระแหน่ เสิร์ฟ

NAM PHRIK LONG RUA LAE-MU WAN
Sweet pork with hot chilli sauce
น้ำพริกลงเรือและหมูหวาน

INGREDIENTS

20 grams peeled garlic cloves

3 tbsp. shrimp paste

5 shredded madan fruits (or 1 green mango)

1-2 tbsp. thinly sliced hot
or ordinary chillies

4-5 tbsp. sugar, 2 tbsp. lime juice

1/2 cup finely ground dried shrimp

1/2 cup sweet pork, 1 salted egg

1/2 cup crumbled crisp fried catfish

1 tbsp. cooking oil

PREPARATION

1. Place the garlic and shrimp paste in a mortar and pound until thoroughly mixed. Add the madan and pound to mix in thoroughly. Add the chilli and just break with pestle. Add the sugar and lime juice.

2. Heat oil in a frying pan and fry the chilli paste. Add the sweet pork and the dried shrimp. Taste and adjust flavor so it is sweet, sour, and salty.

3. Place chilli paste on a serving plate. Cut salted egg into small cubes and sprinkle on the chilli paste together with the crisp fried catfish. Serve with fresh vegetables.

PREPARATION FOR SWEET PORK

Heat 2 tbsp. oil in frying pan. Add 2 tbsp. sugar and stir until fragrant. Add 2 tbsp. fish sauce and slices pork and fry over low heat. Add 2 tbsp. thinly sliced shallots and simmer until pork is cooked and dry.

เครื่องปรุง

กระเทียมปอกเปลือก 20 กรัม กะปิ 3 ช้อนโต๊ะ
มะดันซอย (หรือมะม่วงดิบ 1 ลูก) 5 ผล
พริกขี้หนู หรือพริกเหลืองหั่นบาง ๆ 1-2 ช้อนโต๊ะ
น้ำตาล 4-5 ช้อนโต๊ะ น้ำมะนาว 2 ช้อนโต๊ะ
กุ้งแห้งอย่างดีโขลกละเอียด 1/2 ถ้วย
หมูหวาน 1/2 ถ้วย ไข่เค็ม 1 ฟอง
ปลาดุกฟูกรอบ 1/2 ถ้วย น้ำมัน 1 ช้อนโต๊ะ

วิธีทำ

1. โขลกกระเทียม กะปิเข้าด้วยกันให้ละเอียด ใส่มะ-ดัน โขลกละเอียด ใส่พริกขี้หนูบุบพอแตก ใส่น้ำตาล น้ำมะนาว

2. ใส่น้ำมันลงในกระทะ ตั้งไฟ ใส่น้ำพริก (ส่วนผสมข้อ 1) ลงผัด ใส่กุ้งแห้งและหมูหวาน ผัดให้เข้ากัน ชิมรสให้มี 3 รส หวาน เปรี้ยว เค็ม

3. การจัดเสิร์ฟ ตักน้ำพริกใส่ถ้วย หั่นไข่เค็มเป็นชิ้นสี่เหลี่ยมเล็กๆ โรยหน้าและปลาดุกฟู รับประทานกับผักสด เช่น แตงกวา ถั่วพู ถั่วฝักยาว ผักบุ้ง มะเขือ

วิธีทำหมูหวาน

ใส่น้ำมัน 2 ช้อนโต๊ะ ลงในกระทะ ใส่น้ำตาล 2 ช้อนโต๊ะ ผัดให้หอม ใส่น้ำปลา 2 ช้อนโต๊ะ ใส่เนื้อ-หมูลงผัด เคี่ยวไฟอ่อนๆ ใส่หอมแดง เคี่ยวจนแห้ง ยกลง

NAM PHRIK ONG
Pork and tomato sauce
น้ำพริกอ่อง

INGREDIENTS

3 tbsp. chopped pork

1 cup sliced cherry tomatoes

5 dried chillies, soaked in water

2 tbsp. chopped coriander leaves

3 tbsp. chopped shallots

1 1/2 tsp. chopped garlic cloves

5 cloves garlic

1 tbsp. finely sliced galangal, 1 tsp. salt

1 tsp. shrimp paste or anchovy

1/2 cup water

2 tbsp. cooking oil

Fresh Vegetables : cucumber, string bean, carrot, eggplant, cabbage, etc.

Boiled Vegetables : string bean, eggplant (long), pumpkin vine tip, swamp cabbage, banana blossom, etc.

PREPARATION

1. Pound the chillies, salt, and galangal well in a mortar. Add the onion, shrimp paste or anchovy, and the five garlic cloves and pound to mix thoroughly. Add the pork and continue pounding to mix. Finally, add the tomatoes pound to mix well.

2. Heat the oil in a wok. When it is hot, add the chopped garlic. When the garlic is fragrant, add the pork and tomato chilli paste and continue frying over low heat with stirring, until the ingredients take on a gloss; then, add the water.

3. Continue cooking with regular stirring until much of the water evaporates and the mixture becomes fairly thick. Then, transfer to a bowl, sprinkle with chopped coriander leaves and serve with fresh vegetables or boiled vegetables or both.

เครื่องปรุง

หมูสับ 3 ช้อนโต๊ะ

มะเขือเทศสีดาหั่นชิ้น 1 ถ้วย

พริกแห้งหั่นท่อนสั้นๆ แช่น้ำ 5 เม็ด

ผักชีสับ 2 ช้อนโต๊ะ

หอมแดงสับ 3 ช้อนโต๊ะ

กระเทียมสับ 1 1/2 ช้อนชา

กระเทียม 5 กลีบ

ข่าหั่นละเอียด 1 ช้อนโต๊ะ

เกลือป่น 1 ช้อนชา

กะปิ 1 ช้อนชา

น้ำ 1/2 ถ้วย

น้ำมัน 2 ช้อนโต๊ะ

ผักสด : แตงกวา ถั่วฝักยาว แครอท มะเขือ กะหล่ำปลี ฯลฯ

ผักต้ม : ถั่วฝักยาว มะเขือยาว ยอดฟักทอง ผักบุ้ง หัวปลี ฯลฯ

วิธีทำ

1. โขลกพริกแห้ง เกลือ ข่า เข้าด้วยกันให้ละเอียด แล้วจึงใส่หอมแดง กะปิ และกระเทียม ลงโขลก ให้ละเอียด ใส่เนื้อหมูและมะเขือเทศลงโขลกเป็น อันดับสุดท้าย

2. ใส่น้ำมันลงในกระทะ ตั้งไฟ พอร้อน เจียวกระ-เทียมให้เหลือง มีกลิ่นหอม หรี่ไฟ แล้วตักน้ำพริก ผสมหมู (ส่วนผสมข้อ 1) ใส่กระทะ ผัดต่อจนน้ำ-มันขึ้นเป็นเงา แล้วจึงเติมน้ำ

3. ผัดต่อไปจนน้ำระเหยและน้ำพริกข้น ตักใส่ถ้วย โรยหน้าด้วยผักชี รับประทานได้ทั้งกับผักสดและผัก ต้ม

NAM PHRIK KAPI
Shrimp paste chilli sauce with vegetable
น้ำพริกกะปิ

INGREDIENTS

2 tbsp. shrimp paste, roasted until fragrant
1 tsp. hot chilli, stems removed
1 tbsp. ground dried shrimp
1 tbsp. chopped peeled garlic cloves
2-3 tbsp. sugar
3 tbsp. fish sauce
3 tbsp. lime juice

PREPARATION

1. Place the garlic and shrimp paste in a mortar and pound until thoroughly mixed. Add dried shrimp and pound to mix in. Add hot chilli. Add sugar, fish sauce, and lime juice to taste.

2. Serve with vegetables, such as winged beans, string beans, bamboo shoots, gord gourd leaves, or water mimosa, boiled and topped with coconut cream, or with fresh vegetables, such as cucumbers, eggplant, wing bean, string bean or with cha-om or long eggplant fried with egg.

3. Accompanies fried mackerel.

เครื่องปรุง

กะปิเผาไฟพอหอม 2 ช้อนโต๊ะ
พริกขี้หนูเด็ดก้าน 1 ช้อนชา
กุ้งแห้งป่น 1 ช้อนโต๊ะ
กระเทียมปอกเปลือกซอย 1 ช้อนโต๊ะ
น้ำตาล 2-3 ช้อนโต๊ะ
น้ำปลา 3 ช้อนโต๊ะ
น้ำมะนาว 3 ช้อนโต๊ะ

วิธีทำ

1. โขลกกะปิกับกระเทียมเข้าด้วยกันให้ละเอียด ใส่กุ้งแห้งโขลกรวมกัน ใส่พริกขี้หนู ปรุงรสด้วยน้ำตาล น้ำปลา และน้ำมะนาว ชิมรสตามต้องการ

2. รับประทานกับผักต้มราดกะทิ เช่น ถั่วพู ถั่วฝัก-ยาว หน่อไม้ ตำลึง ผักกระเฉด ฯลฯ หรือผักสดต่างๆ เช่น แตงกวา มะเขือ ถั่วพู ถั่วฝักยาว หรือผักชุบไข่ทอด เช่น ชะอม มะเขือยาว

3. จัดแนมกับน้ำพริก คือปลาทูทอด

LON HAM
Rice picble ham in coconut cream
หลนแฮม

INGREDIENTS

200 grams ham, cut into small cubes (1 cup)

2 cups coconut milk

1/4 cup sliced shallots

1/2 cup fermented rice

6 red, yellow, green spur chillies
cut into short lengths

1 tbsp. sugar

2 tsp. salt

2-3 tbsp. tamarind juice

PREPARATION

Place coconut milk in pot with the ham and fermented rice and heat to boiling. Add salt, tamarind juice, and sugar to taste, then add the shallots and spur chilli. When the sauce comes to a boil, remove from heat. Serve with fresh vegetables,
such as cucumbers, cabbage, white turmeric roots, winged bean, string beans and lettuce.

เครื่องปรุง

แฮมหั่นสี่เหลี่ยมเล็ก ๆ (1ถ้วย) 200 กรัม

กะทิ 2 ถ้วย

หอมแดงซอย 1/4 ถ้วย

ข้าวหมาก 1/2 ถ้วย

พริกชี้ฟ้าเขียว เหลือง แดงหั่นท่อนสั้น 6 เม็ด

น้ำตาล 1 ช้อนโต๊ะ

เกลือป่น 2 ช้อนชา

น้ำมะขามเปียก 2-3 ช้อนโต๊ะ

วิธีทำ

ผสมกะทิกับแฮม ข้าวหมาก ตั้งไฟพอเดือด ใส่เกลือ น้ำมะขามเปียก น้ำตาล ปรุงให้ได้รส 3 รส ใส่หอมแดง พริกชี้ฟ้า พอเดือดอีกครั้ง ยกลง รับ-ประทานกับผักสด เช่น แดงกวา กะหล่ำปลี ขมิ้นขาว ถั่วฝักยาว ฯลฯ

KHANOM JEEN NAM PHRIK

Rice vermicelli and sweet prawn sauce

ขนมจีนน้ำพริก

INGREDIENTS

400 grams prawns, shelled and deveined
1/2 cups swamp cabbage leaves tempura
1/2 cup flower tempura (that can be eat)
1/2 cup sliced banana flower,
soaked in lime juice before served
1/4 cup fried dried chillies
3 3/4 cups coconut milk
7 dried small chillies, 2 tbsp. chopped garlic
50 grams ground roasted shelled mungbean
6 tbsp. sugar, 6 tbsp. fish sauce
6 tbsp. lemon juice, 400 grams rice vermicelli
1/4 cup cooking oil

INGREDIENTS FOR SPICE MIXTURE

1 tbsp. ground dried chilli
2 tbsp. roasted shallot
2 tbsp. roasted garlic, 1 tsp. roasted galangal
1 tbsp. chopped coriander root

PREPARATION

1. Pound the roasted garlic, shallot, galangal, the coriander root in a mortar until well ground and thoroughly mixed.

2. Skim off 1 cup coconut cream. Place coconut cream in a pot and heat until some oil surfaces, remove from heat and set aside.

3. Heat 1 cup of the remaining coconut milk and 1 cup of water to boiling, and add the prawns. When the prawns are done, remove them from the pot, place them in a mortar, and pound well.

4. Add the remaining 1 3/4 cups of co-

เครื่องปรุง

กุ้งปอกเปลือก 400 กรัม
ผักบุ้งชุบแป้งทอด 1/2 ถ้วย
ดอกเข็มชุบแป้งทอด 1/2 ถ้วย
หัวปลีอ่อนหั่นบาง ๆ
(แช่น้ำมะนาวก่อนเสิร์ฟ) 1/2 ถ้วย
พริกแห้งทอด 1/4 ถ้วย
กะทิ 3 3/4 ถ้วย พริกแห้งเม็ดเล็ก 7 เม็ด
กระเทียมสับ 2 ช้อนโต๊ะ
ถั่วเขียวแกะเปลือกคั่วคั่วบด 50 กรัม
น้ำตาล 6 ช้อนโต๊ะ น้ำปลา 6 ช้อนโต๊ะ
น้ำมะนาว 6 ช้อนโต๊ะ ขนมจีน 400 กรัม
น้ำมัน 1/4 ถ้วย

เครื่องปรุงน้ำพริก

พริกป่น 1 ช้อนโต๊ะ หอมแดงเผา 2 ช้อนโต๊ะ
กระเทียมเผา 2 ช้อนโต๊ะ ข่าเผา 1 ช้อนชา
รากผักชีหั่นละเอียด 1 ช้อนโต๊ะ

วิธีทำ

1. ช้อนหัวกะทิไว้ 1 ถ้วย โขลกหอมเผา กระเทียมเผา ข่า รากผักชี เข้าด้วยกันให้ละเอียด

2. เคี่ยวหัวกะทิให้แตกมันมาก ๆ ยกลงพักไว้

3. ต้มกุ้งกับหางกะทิที่เหลือให้สุก ตักกุ้งขึ้นโขลกให้ละเอียด

4. ผสมหัวกะทิและหางกะทิรวมกัน ใส่กะทิผสมลงในกุ้งทีละน้อย ใส่ถั่วป่น ใส่เครื่องที่โขลกและน้ำปลา น้ำตาล ชิมรส เปรี้ยว เค็ม หวาน

5. เจียวกระเทียมในน้ำมัน พอเหลืองตักขึ้น เจียวพริกป่นต่อ (ไฟอ่อน) พอน้ำมันเป็นสีแดง ตักใส่หม้อน้ำพริก ใส่ผักชี กระเทียมเจียว

6. จัดขนมจีน และผักชนิดต่าง ๆ ใส่จานราดด้วยน้ำพริก เสิร์ฟ

conut to the pot in which the prawns were cooked. Add, a little at a time and stirring after each addition, the spice mixture along with the pounded prawns. Then, mix in the mungbeans and add the fish sauce, palm sugar, and lime juice to give the sauce a sour, sweet, and salty taste. When satisfied, remove the pot from the heat.

5. Saute the chopped garlic in the cooking oil. When it begins to brown, remove the garlic from the oil, put the ground dried chilli in, and reduce the heat.

6. When the oil has taken on a red colour, transfer it to the pot containing the sauce, add the coconut milk set aside earlier, and sprinkle with the sauteed garlic.

7. To serve, place four coils of rice vermicelli on each plate, add all vegetables and chilli, and then spoon on about 1/2 cup of the sauce.

KHANOM JEEN NAM YA
Rice vermicelli with fish sauce
ขนมจีนน้ำยา

INGREDIENTS

1 meaty fish (200 grams), 2 hard boiled eggs, each peeled and cut into 15 sections
5 1/2 cups coconut milk
1/2 cup bitter gourd, cut into thin slices and boiled
100 grams string bean, cut into short lengths and boiled a short time
100 grams boiled swamp cabbage, cut into thin slices
100 grams boiled bean sprouts
1/2 cup sweet basil (maenglak)
1 red spur chilli, 2-3 tbsp. fish sauce
1 kg. rice vermicelli, 1 tbsp. ground dried chillies

INGREDIENTS SPICE MIXTURE

3 dried chillies, seeds removed
7 shallots, cut up coarsely, 2 garlic bulbs
1 one-inch thick piece of salted fish, roasted
2 tsp. minced galangal
2 tbsp. sliced lemon grass
1 cup minced krachai, 1 tsp. salt
1 tsp. shrimp paste, 1 cup water

Place all the above in a pot and simmer over low heat until soft. Remove from heat, cool, place in mortar, and pound to a fine paste.

PREPARATION

1. Skim of 1/2 cup coconut cream and set aside to add at the end.
2. Boil fish until done in 1 cup water. Save

เครื่องปรุง

ปลาเนื้อ ๆ 1 ตัว 200 กรัม
ไข่ต้ม 15 นาที 2 ฟอง
กะทิ 5 1/2 ถ้วย
มะระต้มผ่าครึ่งลูกหั่นบาง ๆ 1/2 ถ้วย
ถั่วฝักยาวต้มหั่นสั้น ๆ 100 กรัม
ผักบุ้งต้มหั่น 100 กรัม
ถั่วงอกลวก 100 กรัม
ใบแมงลัก 1 กำเล็ก
พริกชี้ฟ้าแดง 1 เม็ด
น้ำปลา 2-3 ช้อนโต๊ะ
ขนมจีน 1 กิโลกรัม
พริกป่น 1 ช้อนโต๊ะ

เครื่องปรุงน้ำพริก

พริกแห้งแกะเมล็ดออก 3 เม็ด
หอมแดงหั่นหยาบ ๆ 7 หัว
กระเทียม 2 หัว
ปลาเค็มปิ้งหน้า 1 นิ้ว 1 ชิ้น
ข่าหั่นละเอียด 2 ช้อนชา
ตะไคร้หั่น 2 ช้อนโต๊ะ
กระชายหั่นละเอียด 1 ถ้วย
เกลือป่น 1 ช้อนชา
กะปิ 1 ช้อนชา
น้ำ 1 ถ้วย

เตรียมเครื่องปรุงทุกอย่างใส่น้ำตั้งไฟอ่อน
เคี่ยวจนนุ่มยกลง บดให้ละเอียด (ก่อนจะบดปล่อย
ให้เย็นก่อน)

วิธีทำ

1. ช้อนหัวกะทิไว้ 1/2 ถ้วย สำหรับใส่ครั้งสุดท้าย
2. ต้มให้น้ำเดือด 1 ถ้วย ต้มปลาจนสุก เก็บน้ำต้ม
ปลาไว้

the water in which the fish was boiled.

3. Remove the meat from the fish, add to the chilli paste in the mortar, and pound to mix thoroughly. Dip paste into a pot, mix in coconut milk, and heat to boiling. Add the fish broth and fish sauce and simmer, stirring regularly to prevent sticking. When the sauce has thickened and its surface glistens bright red, add the coconut cream and remove from heat.

4. Spoon the hot sauce over the rice vermicelli, vegetables, and boiled egg arranged on plates just before serving.

3. แกะเนื้อปลาบดกับน้ำพริกและน้ำกะทิ ใส่ลงใน หม้อ ตั้งไฟอ่อน ๆ ให้เดือด ใส่น้ำต้มปลา น้ำปลา เคี่ยวไปเรื่อย ๆ หมั่นคนอย่าให้ติดก้นหม้อ พอข้น หอมและมีน้ำมันออกสีแดง ๆ ลอยหน้า ใส่หัวกะทิ ปล่อยให้เดือดอีกครั้ง ยกลง

4. จัดขนมจีน และผักวางข้าง ๆ และไข่ต้ม ราด ด้วยน้ำยา

PHAD THAI KUNG SOD

Fried noodles Thai style

ผัดไทยกุ้งสด

INGREDIENTS

300 grams narrow rice noodles

5 shelled prawns, 3 eggs

500 grams bean sprouts

1 cake soybean curd, cut into small slivers

50 grams Chinese leek leaves, 1 lemon

50 grams chopped pickled white radish

1/2 cup ground roasted peanuts

1 tsp. ground dried chillies

1 tbsp. chopped shallots

1 tbsp. chopped garlic, 4 tbsp. sugar

4 tbsp. tamarind juice or vinegar

3 tbsp. fish sauce, 1/2 cup cooking oil

PREPARATION

1. Heat 3 tbsp. oil in a frying pan and saute garlic and shallots. When yellowed, add noodles with just enough water to soften them and fry, turning constantly with spatula to prevent sticking. Then move noodles to side of pan.

2. Put 3 tbsp. oil into pan. When hot, fry the prawn, pickled white radish, bean curd, and dried chillies, sugar, tamarind juice or vinegar and fish sauce and then return the noodles, mix thoroughly, and move to side.

3. Put 2 tbsp. oil into the pan. When heated, break eggs into pan and scramble with spatula, spreading egg in a thin layer over the pan. When set, return the noodles and mix together. Add half the bean sprouts and the Chinese leek leaves and turn to mix together. spoon onto plates and sprinkle with ground peanuts. Serve with bean sprouts, Chinese leek leaves.

เครื่องปรุง

ก๋วยเตี๋ยวเส้นเล็ก 300 กรัม

กุ้งแกะเปลือก 5 ตัว

ไข่ไก่ 3 ฟอง

ถั่วงอก 500 กรัม

เต้าหู้หั่นเล็กๆ 1 แผ่น

ใบกุยช่าย 50 กรัม

มะนาว 1 ลูก

หัวผักกาดเค็มสับ 50 กรัม

ถั่วลิสงป่น 1/2 ถ้วย

พริกป่น 1 ช้อนชา

หอมแดงสับ 1 ช้อนโต๊ะ

กระเทียมสับ 1 ช้อนโต๊ะ

น้ำตาลทราย 4 ช้อนโต๊ะ

น้ำมะขามเปียกหรือน้ำส้มสายชู 4 ช้อนโต๊ะ

น้ำปลา 3 ช้อนโต๊ะ

น้ำมัน 1/2 ถ้วย

วิธีทำ

1. เจียวหอม กระเทียมกับน้ำมัน 3 ช้อนโต๊ะ ใส่เส้นก๋วยเตี๋ยว ใส่น้ำเล็กน้อยพอให้เส้นนุ่ม ปรุงรส ผัดให้เข้ากันเร็วๆ อย่าให้เส้นเกาะกันเป็นก้อน กันเส้นไว้ข้างกระทะ

2. ใส่น้ำมัน 3 ช้อนโต๊ะ ผัดกุ้ง ผักกาดเค็ม เต้าหู้ พริกป่น น้ำตาล น้ำมะขามเปียก น้ำปลา ตลบเส้นลงมาคลุกให้เข้ากัน กันเส้นไว้ข้างกระทะ

3. ใส่น้ำมัน 2 ช้อนโต๊ะ ต่อยไข่ใส่ กระจายบางๆ แล้วกลับเส้นลงผัดใส่ถั่วงอกครึ่งหนึ่ง ใส่ใบกุยช่าย ตักขึ้น โรยถั่วลิสง ผักที่ใช้รับประทาน ถั่วงอก ต้น-กุยช่าย

MEE KATI
Rice noodles in coconut milk sauce
หมี่กะทิ

INGREDIENTS

250 grams dried thin rice noodles

150 grams chicken or pork

100 grams yellow soy bean curd, 1 egg

300 grams bean sprouts

100 grams Chinese leek leaves

1 1/2 cups coconut cream

2 lemons, sliced into wedges

1/4 coriander leaves plants

2 thinly sliced red spur chillies

1-2 tsp. ground dried chillies

6 finely chopped shallots, 2 tbsp. sugar

1/4 cup fermented soy beans

2 tbsp. tamarind juice, 1-2tbsp.cooking oil

PREPARATION

1. Soak the rice noodles in water 15 minutes to soften, then drain.

2. Slice the chicken or pork into small pieces, cut bean curd into small, thin slices.

3. Wash the bean sprouts and the Chinese leek leaves and cut into 1 inch lengths.

4. Heat 1 tbsp. oil in a frying pan, pour beated egg into pan, spread thinly over bottom of pan. When firm, roll up and cut into long thin strips.

5. Heat coconut milk in a frying pan and add shallots. When fragrant, add chicken or pork, fermented soybeans, sugar, tamarind juice, bean curd, and dried chillies and cook together. Dip up about half the sauce.

6. Put the noodles in the remaining sauce and mix in well. Add the bean sprouts and Chinese leek leaves and mix in, then dip onto plates.

เครื่องปรุง

เส้นหมี่ 250 กรัม เนื้อไก่หรือหมู 150 กรัม
เต้าหู้เหลือง 100 กรัม ไข่ 1 ฟอง
ถั่วงอก 300 กรัม กุยช่าย 100 กรัม
หัวกะทิ 1 1/2 ถ้วย มะนาวผ่าเป็นชิ้น ๆ 2 ผล
ผักชีเด็ดเป็นใบ 1/4 ถ้วย
พริกชี้ฟ้าแดงหั่นฝอย 2 เม็ด พริกป่น 1-2 ช้อนชา
หอมแดงสับละเอียด 6 หัว
น้ำตาลทราย 2 ช้อนโต๊ะ เต้าเจี้ยว 1/4 ถ้วย
น้ำมะขามเปียก 2 ช้อนโต๊ะ น้ำมัน 1-2 ช้อนชา

วิธีทำ

1. แช่เส้นหมี่ในน้ำ 15 นาที ตักขึ้นให้สะเด็ดน้ำ พักไว้

2. หั่นเนื้อไก่หรือเนื้อหมูเป็นชิ้นเล็ก ๆ หั่นเต้าหู้ เหลืองชิ้นเล็ก ๆ บาง ๆ

3. ล้างถั่วงอกกับกุยช่ายหั่นท่อนสั้น 1 นิ้ว ส่วนโคน ตัดยาว ๆ ไว้จัดจาน

4. ใส่น้ำมันลงในกระทะบาง ๆ 1 ช้อนโต๊ะ ต่อยไข่ดี พอเข้ากัน กลอกไข่ใส่กระทะให้เป็นแผ่นบาง ๆ ม้วนแล้วหั่นฝอย

5. ใส่หัวกะทิลงเคี่ยวในกระทะตั้งไฟ ใส่หอมแดงลง ผัดพอหอม ใส่เนื้อไก่หรือเนื้อหมู ใส่เต้าเจี้ยว น้ำตาล น้ำมะขามเปียก เต้าหู้ พริกป่น ผัดให้เข้ากัน ชิมรส ตักขึ้นไว้ครึ่งหนึ่งสำหรับราดหน้า

6. ส่วนที่เหลือใส่เส้นลงผัดให้เข้ากัน ใส่ถั่วงอกและ ใบกุยช่าย ผัดให้เข้ากัน

7. ตักขึ้นจัดใส่จานราดหน้า โรยผักชี พริกชี้ฟ้าแดง รับประทานกับถั่วงอก กุยช่าย หัวปลี

7. Spoon sauce over the noodles top with thinly sliced fried egg, and sprinkle with coriander and red chillies. Serve with bean sprouts, lime wedges, Chinese leek leaves.

PHAD MEE KROB

Crispy sweet and sour rice noodles

ผัดหมี่กรอบ

INGREDIENTS

150 grams very fine thin rice noodles

1/4 cup finely chopped fresh shrimp

1/4 cup finely chopped pork

1 cake yellow soybean curd, cut to match-stick size pieces and fried crisp

3 Chinese leek plants

50 grams bean sprout

2 tbsp. coriander leaves

1 finely sliced red spur chilli

1 tbsp. chopped garlic and shallots

2 pickled garlic bulbs, finely sliced

1 tsp. ground dried chillies

4 tbsp. sugar, 1 tbsp. fish sauce

1 tbsp. lemon juice, 1 tbsp. vinegar

1 tbsp. fermented soybeans,

3 cups cooking oil for frying

เครื่องปรุง

เส้นหมี่ 150 กรัม

กุ้งสดหั่นชิ้นเล็ก ๆ 1/4 ถ้วย

เนื้อหมูหั่นชิ้นเล็ก ๆ 1/4 ถ้วย

เต้าหู้เหลืองหั่นเล็ก ๆ เท่าก้านไม้ขีด

ทอดกรอบ 1 แผ่น

กุยช่าย 3 ต้น ถั่วงอก 50 กรัม

ผักชีเด็ดเป็นใบ 2 ช้อนโต๊ะ

พริกชี้ฟ้าแดงหั่นฝอย 1 เม็ด

กระเทียมและหอมแดงสับ 1 ช้อนโต๊ะ

กระเทียมดองหั่นบาง ๆ 2 หัว

พริกป่น 1 ช้อนชา

น้ำตาล 4 ช้อนโต๊ะ

น้ำปลา 1 ช้อนโต๊ะ

น้ำมะนาว หรือน้ำส้มซ่า 1 ช้อนโต๊ะ

น้ำส้มสายชู 1 ช้อนโต๊ะ

เต้าเจี้ยว 1 ช้อนโต๊ะ

น้ำมันสำหรับทอด 3 ถ้วย

PREPARATION

1. Fry noodles in oil until crisp and golden, then drain.

2. Heat 1/4 cup oil in a frying pan. Fry garlic and shallots until fragrant, then add the pork and shrimp, seasoning with fermented soybeans, vinegar, fish sauce, sugar, and grount dried chillies. When thick, add the lemon juice, mix, taste, and season to obtain sweet, sour, and salty flavor.

3. Reduce heat, add the noodles and continue turning them until they stick together, then add the bean curd and dip onto plates.

4. Sprinkle with the pickled garlic, finely sliced lemon rind, coriander, and red spur chilli and place bean sprouts and Chinese leek leaves on the sides of the plates.

วิธีทำ

1. ทอดเส้นหมี่ให้เหลืองกรอบ ตักขึ้นให้สะเด็ดน้ำมัน

2. ผัดกระเทียมและหอมแดงกับน้ำมัน 1/4 ถ้วยให้หอม ใส่เนื้อหมูและกุ้งลงผัด ปรุงรสด้วยเต้าเจี้ยว น้ำส้ม น้ำปลา น้ำตาล พริกป่น ผัดจนข้นเหนียว ใส่น้ำมะนาว คนให้เข้ากัน ชิมรส 3 รส

3. ใส่เส้นหมี่ลงคลุกไฟอ่อน ๆให้ทั่ว จนเส้นแห้งเกาะกัน ใส่เต้าหู้ จัดใส่จาน

4. โรยกระเทียมดอง ผิวส้มซ่าหั่นละเอียด ผักชี พริกชี้ฟ้าแดง วางถั่วงอกและใบกุยช่ายข้าง ๆ จาน

KHAO MU THOD KRATHIAM PHRIK THAI

Pork marinated in garlic fried and pepper on rice

ข้าวหมูทอดกระเทียมพริกไทย

INGREDIENTS

300 grams pork loin
6 peeled garlic cloves
2 tsp. fried garlic
1 minced coriander root
1/8 tsp. ground pepper
2 tsp. fish sauce
1/2 cup cooking oil

PREPARATION

1. Wash and dry the pork and then cut it into thin slices.

2. Pound the coriander root, garlic, and pepper until well ground and thoroughly mixed. Toss the pork slices in this mixture, add the fish sauce, toss once again, and then set aside to marinate for half an hour.

3. Heat the oil in a wok. When hot, put in the pork and fry golden brown; then. remove from the wok. Place on a plate with rice, and garnish with thin slices of red spur chilli.

เครื่องปรุง

หมูสันนอก 300 กรัม
กระเทียมปอกเปลือก 6 กลีบ
กระเทียมเจียว 2 ช้อนชา
รากผักชีหั่นละเอียด 1 ช้อนชา
พริกไทยป่น 1/8 ช้อนชา
น้ำปลา 2 ช้อนชา
น้ำมัน 1/2 ถ้วย

วิธีทำ

1. ล้างเนื้อหมู ซับให้แห้ง หั่นบาง ๆ

2. โขลกรากผักชี กระเทียม พริกไทย เข้าด้วยกัน คลุกกับหมู ใส่น้ำปลา คลุกเคล้าให้เข้ากัน หมักไว้ 1/2 ชั่วโมง

3. ใส่น้ำมันลงในกระทะ ตั้งไฟพอร้อน ใส่หมู ทอด ให้สุกเหลือง ตักใส่จาน เสิร์ฟกับข้าว โรยด้วย กระเทียมเจียว พริกชี้ฟ้าแดงหั่นแฉลบบาง ๆ

KHAO PHAD KA-PHRAO MU

Spicy pork fried rice on crispy basil leaves

ข้าวผัดกะเพราหมู

INGREDIENTS

2 1/2 cups cooked rice

200 grams ground pork

1/2 cup holy basil leaves

1 red and

1 green spur chilli

3 yellow spur chillies

1 tbsp. garlic

1 tsp. sugar

1 tsp. fish sauce

3 tbsp. cooking oil

1/2 cup oil (for frying the basil leaves)

1 boiled salt egg (optional), shelled and cut in pieces

PREPARATION

1. Heat the 1/2 cup of oil in a wok. When hot, put in the basil leaves, fry until crisp, remove from the oil, and set aside to drain.

2. Pound the yellow chillies and the garlic together until well ground. Cut the red and green chillies diagonally into thin slices.

3. Heat the 3 tbsp. of oil in a wok. When hot, stir fry the yellow chillies-garlic mixture until fragrant; then, put in the pork and stir fry, seasoning with the fish sauce and sugar. Next, add the rice and continue stir frying.

4. When the rice is about done, add the sliced red and green chillies and mix thoroughly.

5. Place the fried basil leaves on a plate, dip the fried rice onto the basil leaves. Serve with salt egg.

เครื่องปรุง

ข้าวสวย 2 1/2 ถ้วย

หมูบด 200 กรัม

กะเพราเด็ดเป็นใบ ๆ 1/2 ถ้วย

พริกชี้ฟ้าเขียวแดง 2 เม็ด

พริกชี้ฟ้าเหลือง 3 เม็ด

กระเทียม 1 ช้อนโต๊ะ

น้ำตาลทราย 1 ช้อนชา

น้ำปลา 1 ช้อนชา

น้ำมัน 3 ช้อนโต๊ะ

น้ำมันสำหรับทอดใบกะเพรา 1/2 ถ้วย

วิธีทำ

1. ใส่น้ำมันลงในกระทะ ตั้งไฟพอร้อน ใส่ใบกะเพรา ทอดพอกรอบ ตักขึ้นให้สะเด็ดน้ำมัน

2. โขลกพริกชี้ฟ้าเหลืองกับกระเทียม เข้าด้วยกันให้ละเอียด

3. ใส่น้ำมันลงในกระทะ 3 ช้อนโต๊ะ ใส่พริกที่โขลก (ส่วนผสมข้อ 2) ผัดให้หอม ใส่เนื้อหมู ผัดพอทั่ว ใส่น้ำปลา น้ำตาล ผัดให้ทั่ว ใส่ข้าว ผัดให้ทั่ว

4. หั่นพริกชี้ฟ้าเขียวแดงหั่นแฉลบบาง ๆ ใส่ในกระทะพอทั่ว

5. แบ่งใบกะเพราทอดใส่จาน ตักข้าวที่ผัดวางข้างบน รับประทานกับไข่เค็ม

KHAO PHAD SEE MUANG
Stir-fried rice with shrimp paste
ข้าวผัดสีม่วง

INGREDIENTS

1 1/2 cups rice (300 grams)

150 grams pork sliced into small pieces

1/4 cup chopped or pounded dried shrimp

1 egg

1/4 shredded madan fruit or cooking apple

6 cucumbers, 2 lemons

2 tbsp. coriander leaves

1 thinly sliced red spur chilli

4 chopped shallots

1 tbsp. finely chopped garlic

1 1/2 tbsp. shrimp paste mixed with

1 tbsp. water, 1 tsp. sugar

1 tbsp. fish sauce 1/4 cup cooking oil

1/2 cup sweet pork (See p.78)

เครื่องปรุง

ข้าวสาร (1 1/2 ถ้วย) 300 กรัม

เนื้อหมูหั่นเล็ก ๆ 150 กรัม

กุ้งแห้งหั่นเล็ก ๆ หรือป่นแล้ว 1/4 ถ้วย

ไข่ไก่ 1 ฟอง

มะดันซอย 1/4 ถ้วย

แตงกวา 6 ผล

มะนาว 2 ผล

ผักชีเด็ดเป็นใบ 2 ช้อนโต๊ะ

พริกชี้ฟ้าแดงหั่นฝอย 1 เม็ด

หอมแดงซอย 4 หัว

กระเทียมสับละเอียด 1 ช้อนโต๊ะ

กะปิดี 1 1/2 ช้อนโต๊ะละลายน้ำ 1 ช้อนโต๊ะ

น้ำตาลทราย 1 ช้อนชา

น้ำปลา 1 ช้อนโต๊ะ น้ำมัน 1/4 ถ้วย

หมูหวาน (ดูหน้า 78) 1/2 ถ้วย

PREPARATION

1. Steam rice, using 2 1/2 cups water, about 40 minutes, then rake to separate grains.

2. Fry garlic until golden then add pork and fry. Add shrimp paste; when fragrant, add sugar, fish sauce, and shrimp and fry, mixing together.

3. Add rice and continue frying. When done, remove from heat, sprinkle with madan and shallots, mix together thoroughly, and remove from pan.

4. Beat the egg. Heat 1 tsp. oil in pan, pour in egg and swirl so egg forms thin layer on bottom of pan. When egg sets, roll up and cut into narrow strips.

5. Scoop rice onto plate and sprinkle with egg, coriander, and red spur chilli. Serve with sliced cucumber and lemon.

วิธีทำ

1. นึ่งข้าวใส่น้ำ 2 1/2 ถ้วย นึ่งประมาณ 40 นาที ซุยข้าวให้กระจาย

2. เจียวกระเทียมให้เหลือง ใส่เนื้อหมูลงผัด ใส่กะปิ ผัดให้หอม ใส่น้ำตาล น้ำปลา กุ้งแห้ง ผัดให้เข้ากัน

3. ใส่ข้าวลงผัด ยกลง โรยมะดัน หอมแดง คลุก ให้เข้ากัน

4. ต่อยไข่ตีให้เข้ากัน ตั้งกระทะใส่น้ำมัน 1 ช้อนชา กลอกไข่บาง ๆ แล้วม้วนกลม ๆ หั่นฝอย

5. ตักข้าวใส่จาน โรยไข่ฝอย ผักชี พริกชี้ฟ้าแดง เสิร์ฟกับแตงกวา มะนาว และหมูหวาน

KHAO PHAD MU REU KUNG SAI KHAI

Fried rice with Pork or shrimp and egg

ข้าวผัดหมูหรือกุ้งใส่ไข่

INGREDIENTS

300 grams (1 1/2 cups) rice (not recently harvested)

150 grams pork (5 shelled prawns)

2 eggs, 100 grams onion

6 cucumbers, 2 limes or lemons

6 spring onions, 2 tbsp. coriander plant

1 red spur chilli, 1 tbsp. sugar

3 tbsp. light soy sauce

2 tbsp. tomato catsup

2 1/2 cups water, 1/4 cup cooking oil

PREPARATION

1. Steam rice in 2 1/2 cups water until done (about 40 minutes) and then stir to separate grains.

2. Cut pork into thin slices and marinate in 1 tbsp. light soy sauce for a short time.

3. Slice onion into 1/2 cm. thick rings.

4. Fry onion in oil. When done, add the pork or shrimp, catsup, sugar, and soy sauce and stir together. Then add the rice and fry. When done, remove from pan.

5. Fry eggs in 1 tbsp. oil, turning and breaking regularly. When done, mix in the rice and season to taste.

6. Cut cucumbers into 1/4 inch thick rings and slice red spur chilli into long shreds.

7. Dip rice onto plates and garnish with chopped coriander and the chilli. Serve with cucumber slices, spring onions, and lemon wedges on side of plate.

เครื่องปรุง

ข้าวสาร (ข้าวเก่า) 300 กรัม (1 1/2 ถ้วย)

เนื้อหมู (หรือกุ้งปอกเปลือก 5 ตัว) 150 กรัม

ไข่ไก่ 2 ฟอง

หอมใหญ่ 100 กรัม

แตงกวา 6 ผล

มะนาว 2 ผล

ต้นหอม 6 ต้น

ผักชีเด็ดเป็นใบ 2 ช้อนโต๊ะ

พริกชี้ฟ้าแดง 1 เม็ด

น้ำตาลทราย 1 ช้อนโต๊ะ

ซีอิ๊วขาว 3 ช้อนโต๊ะ

ซอสมะเขือเทศ 2 ช้อนโต๊ะ

น้ำ 2 1/2 ถ้วย

น้ำมัน 1/4 ถ้วย

วิธีทำ

1. นึ่งข้าวใส่น้ำ 2 1/2 ถ้วย นึ่งประมาณ 40 นาที สุกแล้วซุยให้เม็ดกระจาย

2. หั่นเนื้อหมูชิ้นเล็กๆ ใส่ซีอิ๊วขาว 1 ช้อนโต๊ะ คลุกหมักไว้สักครู่

3. หั่นหอมใหญ่ตามขวางหนา 1/2 ซม.

4. ผัดหอมใหญ่กับน้ำมันพอสุก ใส่เนื้อหมู ซอสมะเขือเทศ น้ำตาล ซีอิ๊วขาว ผัดให้ทั่ว ใส่ข้าวลงผัด ตักขึ้น

5. ใส่น้ำมันลงในกระทะ 1 ช้อนโต๊ะ ต่อยไข่ใส่ กลับไปมาให้ไข่สุกและตัดเป็นชิ้น แล้วคลุกกับข้าวให้ทั่ว ชิมรสตามชอบ

6. หั่นแตงกวาเป็นแว่นหนา 1/4 นิ้ว หั่นพริกชี้ฟ้าแดงเป็นเส้นๆ

7. ตักข้าวใส่จาน โรยผักชี พริกชี้ฟ้าแดง จัดแตงกวา ต้นหอม และมะนาววางข้างๆ